THE GAME OF
TABLE TENNIS

THE GAME OF

Drawings by GUSTAV REHBERGER

TABLE TENNIS

by

DICK MILES

J. B. LIPPINCOTT COMPANY
Philadelphia and New York

To the sport

Contents

Illustrations

Introduction

Before we begin your metamorphosis into a winning table tennis player I thought it would be appropriate to tell you something about myself—how I began playing the game, what I have done with it, and how it has changed during my career. This is not a particularly spellbinding yarn and I shall not try to dramatize it, but if knowing something about me helps create a rapport between us the synopsis is worth setting down.

I began playing table tennis when I was eleven—eleven exactly, for, as a birthday gift, a table tennis table was delivered to our apartment in New York City. I was a very much disappointed boy when I opened that gift, because for three months I had been telling my mother that I wanted a pool table. Whether the pool table was too expensive or whether my mother did not know the difference between the games I never found out. I received the table tennis table with as much enthusiasm as I could have mustered for a box of lollipops. The name of the game was particularly obnoxious to me. When I opened the carton and assembled the pieces I learned that I owned a Tea Table Tennis Table. It seemed demeaning to my manliness.

It is a wonder that I ever tried the game at all, for I spent all my free time in the neighborhood streets in the more appropriate pursuit of a future career in "stickball," "boxball," and "stoopball." These great sports have all but vanished from New York City, and if the fate of the nation depended on it I would not know where to find a batter who could swat a "fluke" with a mopstick from Columbus to Amsterdam Avenues. Nowadays, the automobiles, parked bumper to bumper, stifle the city boys' development, but in the late

1930's cars were a luxury and parking spaces were plentiful. If a man threatened to park in our stickball field—the distance between three manhole covers—we would say, "Would you mind moving it down the street, mister?" There was a kid named Lefty, a gawky, redheaded first baseman, who could ask that question with exactly the right balance between threat and appeal.

Nonetheless, the "Tea Table Tennis" set eventually got stretched out over the dining-room table and pursuit of the white ball soon hypnotized me. Though I did not entirely give up the idea of a stickball career I began spending more and more time at the new game playing anyone who would humor me. I lost, I suppose, as much as I won. When I was twelve I began playing golf. A friend of the family with a fine golf swing sawed down some antique clubs to suit my height and taught me how to pivot and how to "hit down on the irons." My table tennis technique owes much to this early golf coaching. But the long, cold city winters necessarily called a "let" on golf and stickball, and table tennis became my game.

I played it contentedly for two years on my Tea Table Tennis set and then discovered that I was not really playing the game at all. There was a table tennis parlor in the neighborhood, Manhattan's Upper West Side, and I passed it every day when returning home from school. One day I courageously entered and saw that my idea of the game—to outlast your opponent in a monotonous duel of close-to-the-table pings and pongs—was completely wrong. Here, grown men and boys my own age played the game with drives and long-range retrieves and made it really look like a sport. They were even using rubber-faced rackets, which contrasted with my sandpaper bat. The proprietor was a man named Mitch, a tall, gaunt insomniac with what I then imagined to be the world's best backhand. I began frequenting Mitch's place and that sleepless gentleman persuaded me to switch to a rubber bat and often let me play "on the house" after my time was up.

One winter night in 1939 the then world champion, Czechoslovakia's Bohumil Vana, visited Mitch's place. Though Vana did not play, he was awesomely impressive to me. His diminutive frame was enveloped by a huge European greatcoat whose lapels were pulled forward and framed his birdlike face like a giant wreath. Sitting on the edge of the table, one foot touching the floor and the other gracefully dangling, he chatted, answered questions, and all the while nonchalantly drummed out intricate rhythms on the table with a bat and ball. He was wonderful in his foreignness. And (as the success stories say) I never thought as I watched him that nine years later in London I would be playing him for the world title in front of 10,000 spectators.

Though I learned the fundamentals of the game at Mitch's, actually the caliber of the play was not really high there and within a year I had outstripped most of the competition. It remained then to graduate to the Broadway Table Tennis Courts which had served as an incubator for many United States champions. Its two floor-through lofts were sandwiched in the middle floors of a rundown four-story structure at 55th Street and Broadway, but conditions for play were ideal. Moreover, America's best players, such as Sol Schiff and Lou Pagliaro, were in daily attendance. I estimate that between the ages of thirteen and eighteen I played table tennis at the Broadway Courts about thirty hours a week. I have to admit that almost none of this time was spent practicing. Two or three dollars, sometimes five, bet on a match, was enough to simulate competitive play and it would have been unthinkable to play a match without a wager on the outcome. Only later did I learn the value of pure practice—playing particular shots without keeping score.

In 1945, at nineteen, I became the youngest player ever to win the U. S. men's singles title and I went on to break the previous record of three (set by Lou Pagliaro) by winning the title five times consecutively.

In 1947, after a wartime hiatus, international table tennis got going again, and that year the U. S. Table Tennis Association sent a team headed by Lou Pagliaro and me to the World Championships being held in Paris. As a team we reached the finals of the Swaythling Cup (the Davis Cup of table tennis), but in the singles I went down ignominiously before England's Johnny Leach. Nerves, induced by my first World Championships, and a hand-cramp induced by the nerves and the near arctic temperature of the unheated arena, were responsible for my poor showing. The European players were not nearly so good as I had imagined, however, and I was sure I would take the world title the next year.

At London the following year I played the best table tennis I have ever played but it was still not good enough to win that elusive title, World Champion. I lost in the quarter finals to the defending champion, that man in the greatcoat, the Czech Bohumil Vana, after leading 2 games to 1 and then leading again 18–15 in the fifth and deciding game. It was the cruelest loss I had ever suffered, crueler even than the one the following year in the World Championships when I again lost to Leach, this time in the quarter finals, 22–20 in the fifth game.

I never did win the world's men's singles title (no American ever has), but I came very close. When the World Championships were at Dortmund, Germany, in 1959 and the luck of the draw pitted me successively against three Chinese players, I beat the first two and in the semifinals (no American has ever gone farther) I narrowly missed beating the third, Jung Kuo-tuan, the eventual winner, in a five-game thriller in which I led most of the way.

The years between my first World Championships competition in 1947 and the present have seen many changes in the sport. The most radical occurred in 1952 when, at the World Championships in Bombay, a relatively unknown Japanese player, Satoh, won the singles title using a newfangled racket that was covered with a layer of sponge rubber on either side rather than with the normal hard, pimpled rubber that all tournament players used. With the sponge bat Satoh was able to achieve spins and speed that were completely unsolvable for the world's best players. Because of the naïveté of their rules, the International Association had never restricted the racket in terms of size, shape, or material, and Satoh's victory caused, within three years, almost every player in the world to switch to sponge rubber. A belated attempt to ban the bat failed.

No one really liked to play with the sponge bat because its extreme liveliness caused many errors. But this loss of control was counterbalanced by the fact that when a player's shot went on the table his opponent had a far more difficult time returning it. Even simple push shots that could have been handled automatically had they been hit with a normal bat became problems when they were hit off sponge rubber. Moreover, the extra speed generated by the sponge lent itself more favorably to attacking play rather than to defense, and table tennis soon became a game of counter-driving attacking players who imagined the only way to win was to hit harder and faster than their opponents. Previously it had been felt that defense was just as important as attack.

It was, incidentally, the clashes between the defensive players—

such as the great Richard Bergmann, four times world champion, and Johnny Leach, twice world champion—and the attackers, such as Bohumil Vana or Hungary's Ferenc Sido, that made table tennis a great spectator sport. Many experts felt that the game lost much of its eye appeal when these duels between opposing styles disappeared after use of the sponge bat became common. Recently, however, there have been some notable successes scored by defensive players using old-fashioned pimpled rubber, particularly Eberhard Scholer of Germany, and it appears likely that this will cause some emulation and that thus the balance may turn a bit toward defensive play.

Another significant change in the game was the hegemony established by the Oriental players. Traditionally, the game had been dominated by the Hungarians and the Czechs; but, after 1952, first the Japanese and then the Chinese began walking off with all the major titles. This was not due to anything connected with the sponge bat, either; for, while the Japanese men players, Tanaka and Ogimura, were winning world titles with their sponge bats, the Japanese women, Eguchi and Watanabe, proved that they were equally capable of dominating their division with normal pimpled rubber. Two things make the Orientals great: first, sound strokes, which the Europeans and Americans neglected when they discovered the potency of the sponge bat, and, second, an enormous number of players. There are 6,000,000 tournament players in China, for example, and their three-time world champion, Chuang Tse-tung, is a national hero. In Japan there are three million players. In contrast, the United States has, currently, five thousand players.

Along with the changes of style in table tennis and the ascendancy of the Orientals there was also a vast increase in international competition. Before World War I about sixteen countries normally competed in the World Championships which were held every year. Nowadays, fifty-five or more countries send 600 players to the event that lasts ten days and must, because of its magnitude and expense, be held biennially. The International Table Tennis Federation, with 104 member nations, is perhaps the largest sports federation in the world.

Well, all this is not meant to frighten you. Few of you, even with the aid of this book, will ever play in the World Championships. But I do want to emphasize that despite the lack of publicity in this country table tennis is, worldwide, almost as important as big-league baseball here or soccer in Europe. In the Far East table tennis is the number-one sport.

Despite the relatively few serious players in the United States there are millions of addicts whom we experts describe as "base-ment players." These are the players who regularly after dinner descend to the basement game room and compete as fiercely with their friends and family as I might compete in the World Champion-ships. But there the similarity between the amateur and the expert ends. Practically speaking, they play different games—the expert plays table tennis as a sport; the basement player is, for the most part, piddling at ping pong. In no other sport is the difference between amateur and expert so great. In golf or tennis or even bowling the duffer at least has some notion of how the expert swings and looks in action because he has seen him in person or on television. But the sport of table tennis and the techniques of its champions are still to be discovered by our basement players.

This book is intended primarily to narrow the gap between amateur players and serious tournament players by illustrating and describing the strokes and techniques used in championship play. No attempt has been made to simplify the explanations of the strokes in the hope that the amateur will get the general idea of what he is supposed to do. Nowhere in the book, for example, have I urged such platitudes as, "keep your eye on the ball" or "practice as much as possible." Knowing full well that the average person, either through private instruction or by following a course in a book, can only get a portion of what is involved, I have endeavored to make my explanations full and detailed in the hope that the portion the reader comes away with will be that much greater.

This book will be extremely valuable too, I believe, to inter-mediate and advanced players. For in illustrating the sport's tech-niques I have tried to show not merely my own method of play but the basic principles of the game—the principles that govern the techniques of the game's masters. In describing the forehand drive, for example, I have tried to show that whether one plays with the Oriental penholder grip or the Western shakehands grip, there are principles common to both that must be adhered to. By re-analyzing his strokes in this light the intermediate or advanced player may well find a panacea for perpetually missing set-ups or losing deuce games.

THE GAME OF
TABLE TENNIS

CHAPTER 1

The Preliminaries

Choosing a Racket

Almost everyone has seen an ordinary table tennis racket which is simply a piece of 3- or 5-ply wood covered on both sides with a layer of rubber pips. Until the introduction of the sponge bat in 1952 this normal rubber-covered bat was almost the only type seen in tournament play. There were one or two tournament players who tried to use a sandpaper-covered bat or even a plain uncovered wooden bat, but these were eccentrics and not very good players. The only variations one normally saw in the rackets of various players were in the shape, the hardness of the rubber pips, and the number of plies of the wood. The weight varied between 4½ and 5¾ ounces.

This "normal rubber" racket, as we call it, is still used by some international experts and there are indications of a revival of interest in it. The overwhelming majority of tournament players nowadays, however, use a bat that is covered with sponge rubber instead of the old-fashioned normal rubber. The layer of sponge is usually about 2 millimeters thick and its playing surface may be covered with rubber pips (like normal rubber) or may be flat with a grippy, rubber finish.

The flat-surfaced sponge rubber bat is called an "inverted" bat because there is, actually, a layer of pips lying face downward. The sponge rubber bat that has a pip-covered surface facing upward on top is called a "sandwich" bat.

One can become a champion using any of the above rackets. Chuang Tse-tung, China's three-time world champion, uses the sandwich racket; two-time world champion Ogimura, of Japan, uses the inverted bat; and China's defensive wizard, Chang Shih-lin, uses a normal pimpled-rubber bat.

The main differences between the rackets are:

The *inverted sponge* imparts a great deal of spin to the ball plus an enormous amount of speed, all with a minimum effort. When the ball contacts the sponge rubber it sinks in somewhat before it rebounds and is then more or less catapulted off the racket surface. Of the three types of bat the inverted, because of its speed and spin, is the most unpredictable and the hardest to control.

The *sandwich sponge* with its pips face up is somewhat slower than the inverted bat and more obedient as far as spin is concerned. It follows, thus, that the player using a sandwich racket has more control, but this is offset by the fact that his shots are less potent and he has to work harder and be more skillful to score points. Still, as I have said, Chuang Tse-tung uses the sandwich bat and seems to get by.

The *normal rubber* bat is the most difficult of all to use. Since its rubber is harder and much less resilient than the sponge rubber there is almost no catapult action at the moment of impact and thus the effortless speed of the sponge bat is not present. Because of this, pimpled normal rubber is now used only by defensive players who attempt to let the spongers beat themselves through their own errors rather than fight them for the attack. The normal rubber bat gives by far the best control, but to be potent with it a player must have sound strokes.

Despite the difficulties of control in the use of the inverted bat, that is the bat I recommend. If I were coaching a twelve-year-old boy, a good athlete, in the hope of turning out a world champion, I would start him off using the inverted sponge . . . not have him build up to it.

For the average home player a switch to inverted sponge will possibly result in some unaccountable losses at first, but only for a few hours. After that, I can promise some astounding victories as the variety of spins and speed will dazzle opponents who may have been unbeatable before.

A normal rubber bat may be used for several years, but sponge bats lose their resiliency much sooner and should be replaced at least twice a year (experts replace theirs every month). The racket should be kept in a dry place, covered, and before every playing session it should be wiped clean with a rag dipped in alcohol or lighter fluid.

Choosing a Table

A large variety of tables is available today . . . almost all of them quite adequate for the full enjoyment of the game. Plywood tables are losing their popularity to tables made of pressed wood, which give, if anything, a truer and faster bounce. If you do choose a plywood table, make sure that it has a 5-ply, ¾-inch top rather than the slower 3-ply, ½-inch top.

The table must be 9 feet long by 5 feet wide, and the playing surface must be 30 inches from the floor. Some manufacturers put their tables on wheels for easier moving and when that is the case check the height of the table before you buy it, since occasionally the wheels are added apparently as an afterthought, thus raising the actual height of the table.

A new table will normally "rub"—that is, the ball will pick up green paint for a time. This will lessen as the paint gets harder but don't try to hasten the process. Under no circumstances should a table tennis table ever be polished with wax or anything other than a damp rag. A polished table becomes slick and causes a spinning ball to skid rather than grip.

Lighting

Have as much light over the table as possible—it's as simple as that. Ideally, two 300-watt bulbs are placed in 14-inch reflectors and hung about 8 feet over the playing surface, centered over each half of the table. Additionally, one 300-watt bulb and reflector should be suspended about 4 feet behind each end of the table to light the back court and these should be hung 2 feet higher than the lights over the table. To avoid glare use the G.E. "Silver Bowl" bottom bulbs. Fluorescent lighting is generally poor for table tennis as it causes a flickering, or stroboscopic, effect.

Balls

The English consistently make the best balls. The very best grades of German and Japanese balls are as good as English balls. American balls are less consistent in quality.

To test the quality of a ball, spin it on a flat surface. If it wobbles it is not round and will not play well. If it passes this first test for roundness, squeeze it in the middle on either side of the seam with your thumb and forefinger. If it gives evenly it is a good ball.

What to Wear

Tennis shoes, white wool or cotton socks, shorts, and a short-sleeved polo shirt are the standard tournament attire. The rules prohibit the wearing of light-colored shirts or shorts (lest the ball be invisible against this background), so gray flannel shorts and navy blue shirts are customary.

I strongly urge beginners to dress for the game every time they play. Tennis shoes, of course, are essential, but it seems worthwhile, too, to change to shorts and polo shirt even though at the beginning you may not be moving around enough to perspire. But, psychologically, the act of changing clothes for the game is beneficial because you will feel more athletic and the extra effort you have invested will stimulate you to try harder.

With these fundamentals out of the way we can begin. Ready, then? Change your clothes, turn the lights on over the table, and take up your racket. From here on I envy you. You will be learning a great sport that will keep you trim and vigorous until you are ninety.

I recommend, incidentally, that if possible you follow the course in this book using the buddy system—that is, learning with a partner of your own ability. This will enable you to practice the techniques without that feeling of competitiveness which inhibits progress.

CHAPTER 2

The Grip—and Spin

Sound strokes begin with a proper grip. Of all racket sports, table tennis is played with the smallest ball and racket and has the smallest target. Therefore, the angle at which the racket is presented to the ball during the swing must be controlled with absolute precision. Small deviations from the correct grip on the racket magnify themselves into gross errors in shotmaking and often into errors of stroke production as well. What happens is that a player with a poor grip is forced, by however much his grip is faulty, to compensate for this deficiency by altering his stroke in some way. In table tennis, just as in golf or tennis, grip and stroke must go together, and while the best grip may not insure the best strokes, a poor grip absolutely forces poor strokes.

Ideally, the best grip would be one which would place the bat in the hand comfortably and securely and allow the player to execute sound strokes without any shifting of the bat in the hand when changing from backhand to forehand and from defense to attack. Paradoxically, in modern table tennis, the best players in the world, the Orientals, have not adopted anything like an all-round grip. Rather, they have instead adopted the so-called penholder grip, which is an unthinkably poor grip for every stroke in the game except one, the forehand drive. But, on the other hand, the penholder grip is so ideal for this attacking shot that the Orientals have made the forehand drive the basis of their style and rely on this weapon almost exclusively during their matches. Rarely, and only as a last resort in an emergency, will the typical Oriental player retreat from the table to play defense—and then only for a chance shot in a rally, followed immediately by a rush back toward the table to again attack with his forehand drive. Thus, the Oriental penholder grip, unsuitable for defensive play backhand or forehand and equally unsuitable for the backhand drive, has determined their all-out attacking style using only the forehand drive. With this one weapon, coupled with their incredibly agile footwork that allows them to hit with their forehand drives shots that would be more natural to take with the backhand, they have gained and maintained ascendancy in the modern game.

There are recent signs, however, that the customary western grip, the "shakehands" grip, is being experimented with successfully even in the Far East. A recent Japanese world champion is a shakehands player as are some new high-ranking players among the Chinese.

It is my opinion that the shakehands grip—the tennis grip—is superior to the penholder grip in that it gives the player more ways of winning in a match, either through attack or defense. Additionally, it does not require a player to maintain so fast a pace as the penholder grip demands. With the penholder grip the player is constantly running to avoid hitting the ball with his backhand, made weak by a grip that forces a poor stroke. (Incidentally, the Far Eastern players use only one side of their rackets, the forehand side. The backhand side of their bats is seldom covered with rubber.) Thus it is the shakehands grip that I am going to recommend and I am going to describe it in some detail. There is much more to the grip than, as some coaches or books say, simply "shaking hands with the bat."

The *shakehands grip* is formed as follows: Holding the head of the bat with the left hand, place the handle of the bat into the open palm as in Figure 1. The handle, you will see, crosses the palm almost at a right angle with the fingers. Now, with the left hand still holding the head of the bat, push the blade down until the throat of the bat fits firmly and snugly into the web between the thumb and forefinger. By pushing downward with the left hand, the right hand will fit up as high as possible into the throat of the blade.

Now close the fingers securely around the handle of the bat until you have the grip shown in Figure 2a. The thumb should be in the center of the blade, pointing upward to the top of the bat. I curl the thumb up slightly with tension which adds a certain firmness and reinforcement for the backhand strokes.

The forefinger lies extended and flat along the other side of the

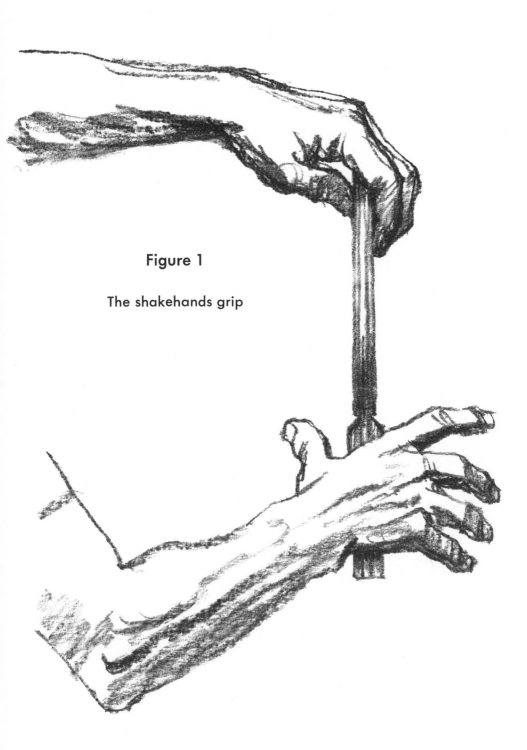

Figure 1

The shakehands grip

Figure 2

The correct shakehands grip

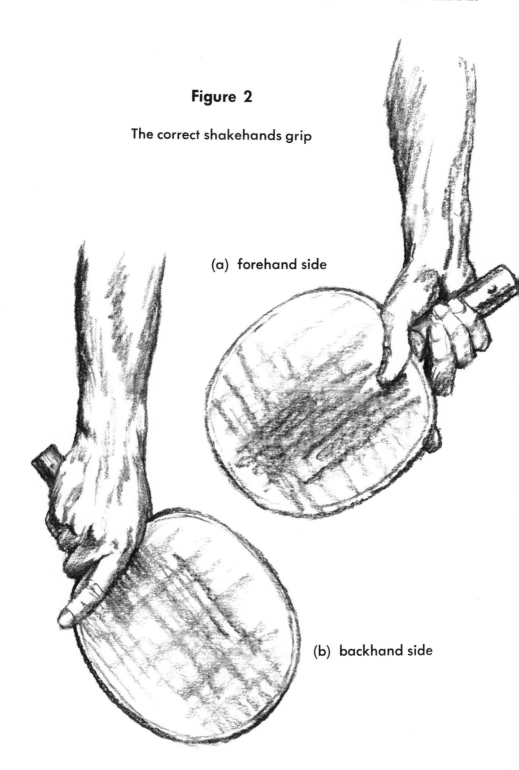

(a) forehand side

(b) backhand side

bat as in Figure 2*b* and, unlike the thumb, it is relaxed. It may extend beyond the edge of the blade of the bat but should never be curled around it. If your forefinger is longer than average, slide it upward along the blade so that more of it is resting against the bat.

Your other three fingers should be gripping the handle as shown in Figure 2*a*. Notice that in an attempt to get my hand higher into the blade I allow my middle finger to slightly overlap the fourth finger. In my grip this finger has the least tension of any. Actually, I hold the bat tightly only with the last two fingers, using the thumb and index fingers mainly as a brace to keep the bat from swerving from its position in the web. By maintaining the tension in the last two fingers in my grip I free the upper part of the bat, the head, to swing more freely, like the head of a hammer.

Here is a good test to see whether you have formed the correct grip. If you hold the bat directly in front of you, with the face of the blade up like a saucer and an imaginary extension of the handle pointed toward the center of your chest, the angle formed by your bat, wrist, and forearm should be that shown in Figure 3*a*. You will notice in this drawing that the back of the hand and the forearm are not lined up so that the bat becomes an extension of the arm. This is a crucial point. In table tennis the bat is *never* used as an extension of the arm; for the bat must move from the wrist, not from the arm.

Unfortunately, the most common faulty deviation from this correct grip is the one that leads to the worst problems in developing the most important shot in the game—the forehand drive. The deviation is this: when the handle is not held securely by the last two fingers the blade may slip clockwise in the hand so that some part of the palp of the right thumb comes to rest against the rubber surface of the bat. This can happen, for example, if the handle is slippery or shellacked, or if the hand is perspiring, and the thumb exerts pressure against the blade which forces it to turn. (Figure 3*b* shows the wrong grip.)

When this faulty grip occurs, a number of things ensue—all of them bad. First, this clockwise turning of the blade in the web of the hand changes the angle of the bat so that it becomes more like an extension of the forearm. (This grip is good for only one shot in the game, the backhand drive, and indeed some players during the course of changing from forehand to backhand during a point

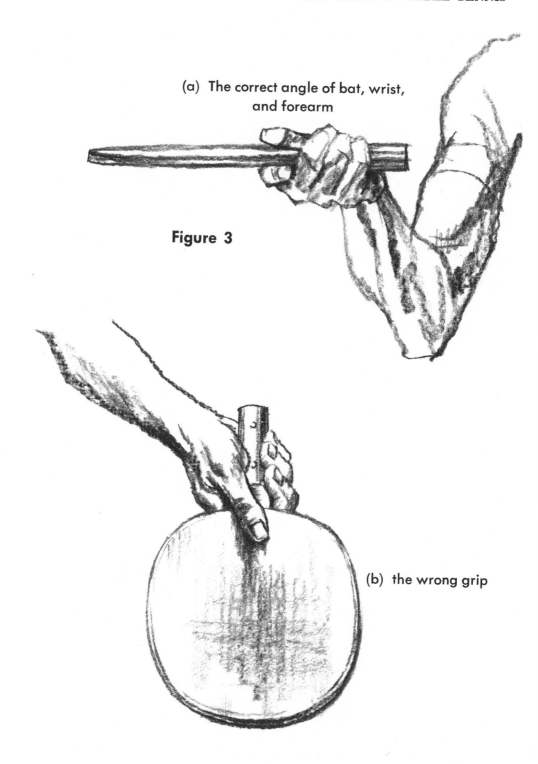

(a) The correct angle of bat, wrist, and forearm

Figure 3

(b) the wrong grip

switch to it with success. But I do not recommend it. To avoid this error in the grip make sure that *at all times* the thumb is resting at right angles to the blade.

Attention, experts! Here is a small experiment to see whether the problems with your forehand drive are not connected with a faulty grip.

Place the bat in your hand with the correct grip as shown in Figure 2a. Now, with your left hand gripping the head of the bat, twist the blade from left to right and at the same time allow the handle to slip in your hand. The blade should rotate in your hand about two inches until it is prevented from further rotation by the knuckle of the forefinger. The thumb, you will see, is now resting with its palp against the rubber. Is your grip anything like this? If it is, it is a backhand grip and you will surely never be able to hit a forehand with it, as I shall explain in the chapter on the forehand attack. Now, with the left hand still holding the head of the bat, reverse the rotation, this time twisting from right to left until the pressure of the throat of the racket against the thumb knuckle forces the thumb off the blade. Stop, squeeze the handle firmly until the thumb once more rests against the blade with the thumbnail at right angles to it. This is the ideal grip for both forehand and backhand defensive shots and particularly for the forehand drive.

Spin

To understand championship technique the first thing one must grasp is that table tennis is a game of spin. When spin is applied to the light celluloid ball its air resistance is increased and its flight is altered. The expert uses this principle, and every shot he makes is controlled by imparting spin to the ball. Unlike tennis, in which the volleys and the overhead smashes are usually hit flat, in table tennis all shots, from the slow, close-to-the-table push returns to the 120-mph kill of a setup, require the use of spin.

Curiously enough, though the expert has a wide range of choice in the *amount* of spin he uses and will vary it with the particular shot, the *type* of spin he uses is extremely limited—limited, in fact, to two. He may use either *underspin* or *overspin* but never *sidespin*. Moreover, he may not even combine sidespin into his shots. Attempting fancy sidespin shots is the dead giveaway of a duffer.

Overspin—rotating the ball *toward* your opponent—is called topspin. Topspin must be used on every attacking shot since this forces the ball downward as it crosses the net, thus keeping the hard-hit shots from flying off the end of the table.

Underspin—rotating the ball *away* from your opponent—is called chop. Chop must be used on every defensive shot since it helps to suspend the ball and keep it traveling on a straight course. A defensive shot made from fifteen feet behind the table—the distance an expert is often forced to retreat to—would have little chance of falling onto the table safely unless its loft were maintained by chop.

Though the primary function of spin is to regulate the ball's trajectory, it often acts as a direct point-winner by forcing your opponent to commit an error. This is particularly true in the defensive shots where the effect of your chop, as the ball rebounds from your opponent's racket, is to force the ball downward. Unless your opponent compensates for your spin by angling his racket higher, his return will go into the net. On the attacking shots, however, speed more often than spin forces the error.

Since spin—topspin or chop—must be imparted to the ball on every shot, the path that the racket takes in applying the spin—the swing, or the "stroke," as we experts call it—is crucial. The soundness of a stroke is determined by how consistently and how potently it works. Consistency requires a natural, fluid motion that can be "grooved." Potency requires a motion that will deliver maximum power with minimum effort—even when the ball is being hit softly.

In table tennis, even with a sound stroke, as the ball is hit harder or spun more vigorously, there is a corresponding diminishment of control, and so the player must decide, on every shot, how much control he is willing to sacrifice for an attempt to win the point by forcing the issue. His "percentage" decides victory or defeat. The player handicapped with poor strokes rarely finds the percentage working in his favor.

First Solo Exercise

Though table tennis is a game in which every stroke is played with spin, either topspin for attack or underspin for defense, I am going to ask you to spend a little time with an exercise that has nothing to do with spin. It is an exercise that is seemingly simple at first glance, yet is actually very difficult to master. Once perfected, however, it can lead to rapid progress in the development of the strokes—much more rapid progress than if you were to tackle the strokes without having first attempted this exercise. For the beginner, this little drill in ball control will go more slowly than for the average player, but since his habits are less firmly fixed he may well end up doing it better than the expert. Average players and tournament players should pay close attention here because this exercise involves ball control by use of the wrist—and it is here that most errors in stroke production occur.

Your feet are spread about eight to ten inches apart, with the toes pointed slightly outward. Your weight is evenly balanced and you are relaxed, with the knees bent slightly forward and the shoulders in a loose crouch. Your left arm is held loosely in front of you so that the left hand is *higher* than the elbow. (I place great emphasis, as you will see, on the importance of keeping the left hand up for balance on all shots.) The upper part of your right arm is hanging free, without tension, from the shoulder and your right elbow is resting against your waist close to your hip.

Your right forearm is pointed slightly upward and the forehand side of your bat (thumb side) is face up. Your wrist is bent back slightly so that an angle is formed between the back of the hand and the forearm. Your bat is held perfectly flat, face up. The ball is held in your left hand.

Your object is merely to bounce the ball on your racket, straight up, to a height of eight to ten inches for, let's say, twenty-five continuous hits. Seems easy enough, doesn't it? But the exercise is wasted if it is not done correctly and here is how it must be done.

Since this is an exercise in hand control the ball must be hit with the hand moving the head of the bat into the ball. So, as you tap it into the air remember that the important thing is to keep the wrist flexible. As the ball descends, the wrist comes up to meet it. The right elbow remains against the side and the forearm moves very, very slightly. *Under no circumstances should the wrist be held rigid and the forearm raised to hit the ball.* Table tennis must be played with a supple, though never limp, wrist and the time to cultivate this control is right at the beginning. Mind you do not slap the ball upward. It is only a slight tapping movement of the wrist that sends the ball up. The wrist should never be flipped so far upward that the back of the hand becomes parallel with the forearm.

This, I assure you, is a difficult exercise to master. Start off slowly, perhaps by dropping the ball onto the bat with the left hand and hitting it up only once and then catching it again. When you have mastered this stroke, for this movement of the wrist is really a stroke, try to hit two or three shots successively this way. The emphasis is on rhythm and control, and as you master it you will find that you have to move your feet less and less. Ideally, for this exercise, you should not move your feet at all. The sound of the ball should be metronomic.

A suggestion. Just before the moment of impact, as the ball is descending, you should have the feeling that your forefinger lying along the bottom side of the racket blade exerts a slight upward pressure which is driving the head of the bat toward the ball.

A warning. Don't compromise. If you have difficulty at first in controlling this stroke, do not try to make it easier for yourself by allowing the wrist to become rigid and your control to shift upward to your forearm. The hand must hit the ball!

It may be that after you have practiced the exercise a bit you will notice a slight soreness in your forearm, which comes from exercising a muscle probably not used before. As this forearm muscle develops (see Figure 4) the soreness will disappear.

One of the things you will notice if you analyze the little wrist stroke that is required to do this exercise is that the movement of the head of the bat is faster than that of the wrist, and that the movement of the wrist is faster than that of the forearm (which in this case is very slight), and that the movement of the forearm is faster than that of the upper arm. As you progress in skill and develop proper strokes you will find that all of them (except the pushing strokes close to the table) follow this principle of having the fastest motion at the head of the bat. In all strokes the racket head, in the same time, must cover more distance than the forearm or upper arm and thus it moves faster. The racket head is given this extra speed by being accelerated by the hand.

About Practice

What I am trying to do in this book is illustrate the principles of correct technique for the sport. At the highest level of international competition titles are not won with gimmicks such as fancy serves. They are won with sound strokes that are grooved.

Figure 4

Forearm development

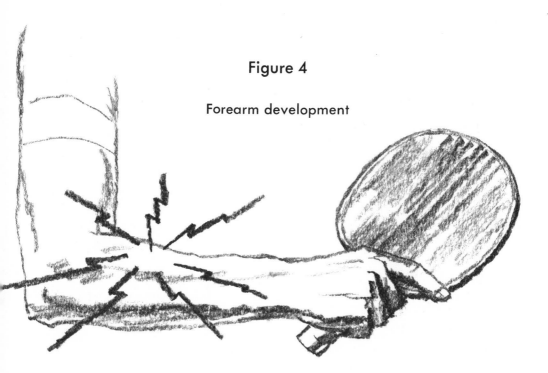

You have in this book all the material with which to become a world champion. But however sound the principles that I give you may be, or however well understood they may be, without practice your domain will be the basement table. Some people are quite content to be the king of the basement table, but for those others who aspire to the thrill of competition and the glory of trophies I must say that only practice can bring about your chance.

Practice, practice, practice! Nothing is more important. The more the better. For the aspiring tournament player, the player who feels the bug of the game and love of competition kindling in his veins, the quicker he comes up out of the basement and joins the nearest league or club the better. For it is there that his losses will stimulate the desire to practice.

In all fairness I cannot suggest any specific practice method as being the best. The Swedes, who are now among the best in the world —indeed, the 1971 World Singles Champion, Stellan Bengtsson, is Swedish—spend as much time doing roadwork and calisthenics as they do at the table; the Japanese listen to lectures from their coaches and spend most of their practice sessions exchanging medium-speed counter-drives; the Czechs lift weights.

For myself I have always tried to practice by setting severe tests for myself—tests that are beyond what I might expect to meet in any match. For instance, as one method of practicing my forehand drive I put my left arm behind my back and grip my right arm at the elbow joint, keeping it locked in close to my right hip. In this awkward position I then spend an hour trying to hit my forehand drive. By locking the right elbow close to my hip what I am doing, in effect, is preventing myself from "reaching" on any shot. By thus limiting my stretch I have to compensate for it by improving my footwork and timing, since the right forearm becomes a shorter lever. Try it!

Another gimmick I have tried is to place a quarter on the table and try with my forehand drive or chop to hit it. I hit it only rarely, but the discipline involved has improved, I imagine, my overall control.

The use of the wall or half of a table-tennis table as a backboard will be described later, and for defensive practice I can think of nothing better unless it be the robot.

Ah! The robot! How I wish it had been available when I was learning the game. The Stiga Robot, as it is properly called, is a recently invented practicing machine from Sweden that is placed at one end of the table and shoots out across the net any chop or drive that one sets its dials for. It can serve, loop-drive, chop, and will alternate its returns, if commanded, from one spot on the table to another. A trough that can hold up to 400 table-tennis balls sits atop a long tube. The tube, in turn, leads to a set of spinning wheels that can be set according to speed and direction desired. The balls feed continuously into the tube and are projected across the net by the spinning wheels. The player, depending upon his skill, can select the amount of speed and spin he wants to practice against and the robot complies.

There is no stronger opponent or finer sportsman than the Stiga Robot. The price of the robot is around $300 and it can be obtained from Stiga Sports, Tranås, Sweden.

CHAPTER 3

The Table Game

The so-called half volley, or push, is the most elementary stroke in the game, yet the one used most often, even among experts. It is the simple shot used in answer to a defensive return from your opponent when for some reason this return does not afford the opportunity to attack. The half volley is the shot we use when we are close to the table and jockeying for position with our opponent, who may likewise be using the half volley. Experts rarely miss when using the half volley, and when two stubborn and careful players oppose each other a "pushing duel" sometimes ensues. Before the "expedite," or time-limit, rule was introduced, these pushing duels were interminable, boring affairs. One such match, in the World Championships at Prague in 1937, lasted seven hours, and one single point of that match lasted two hours and twelve minutes!

Although the push, as you can see, is not a point-winning stroke, it is a necessary part of your stroke equipment as it often decides the winner of a match. Since it is a stroke played only for safety, an error is all the more costly, ending the point before you have had the chance to score on either attack or defense. Missing a half volley in table tennis is like double-faulting in tennis.

The main reason, however, for learning a sound half-volley stroke is that it is really a miniature of the defensive strokes, the chops forehand and backhand, which will become the backbone of your defense.

The Ready Position

The theme of this book, as you have begun to see, is good form, and this begins even before you stroke your racket toward a ball. Actually, it begins as you wait for the ball to cross the net toward you—or even while waiting for your opponent to serve the ball. There is a proper form for this waiting position and observing it will determine to a degree the quality of the stroke that follows.

Figure 5a shows the ready position for executing the half volley, backhand or forehand. Let's analyze the illustration and pick out the crucial elements.

Your feet are about as far apart as the width of your shoulders, toes pointed slightly outward. Your weight is carried slightly forward, but evenly distributed over the flat surface of the feet. Your knees are bent slightly forward, which gives the feeling that you are sitting down a bit. You are relaxed but alert, and the weight of your upper torso and arms hangs from shoulders that are slightly slouched and concave. You are holding the racket in front of you, waist high and extended out about eight inches. The faces of the blade are perpendicular to the table surface. The handle of the bat is pointed slightly downward which, in turn, points the head of the bat slightly upward—a crucial point. From the elbow, which is held in front of the body, the forearm is angled toward the left so that there is a slight angle (most crucial) formed by the wrist and forearm. You are standing about two feet behind the table so that by extending your right arm toward the table your racket head will just touch it. You can move to the left or right with equal ease. The left hand is held high.

Okay, relax a minute. Tie your shoelace, perhaps. Then reassume the ready position and recheck the illustration to see how close you come to including all the crucial elements. To play the game as the champions do you will have to start looking like a champion right at the beginning. Practice taking the ready position until it feels natural. Pay particular attention to the upward angle of the head of the bat, the curve in the wrist, and the height of the left hand. The left hand is always carried so that it is higher than the elbow.

The Backhand Half Volley

After this elaborate description of the basic ready position I think you will find the stroke for the backhand push relatively simple.

Indeed, if you now go astray it will be because you are trying to add things to the stroke rather than keeping it simple.

The stroke for the backhand push consists, as do all strokes in the game, of a backswing, which is used for timing and gaining momentum for power, and a forward swing, which takes the racket into the ball. Let us assume that your opponent has served the ball gently toward you and it is directed down the center of the table straight at you. The backhand push is called for.

Figure 5*b* shows the beginning of the backswing for the backhand push. Actually, this is not so much a swing as it is a drawing back of the racket. This motion is initiated by a pulling back together of the racket, wrist, and forearm by swiveling the forearm in the elbow socket. The bat is taken back horizontally, smoothly and unhurriedly, toward your body until it almost touches the waist.

As the racket is drawn back, the angle of the blade gradually opens, so it seems that if the ball is struck with the bat at this angle it will be hit upward and carry underspin. Indeed, this is just what is supposed to happen.

Figure 5*c* shows the full backswing position for the backhand push. The backswing, mind you, is part of the entire stroke, not a separate action in itself. There will be no pause, therefore, in the swing from the time you begin the backswing until the end of the follow-through.

The backswing, as I have said, is necessary for correct timing. It enables you, before committing yourself to contacting the ball, to enter into the rhythm of the ball's flight. You will learn, through practice, to automatically imagine an ideal contact point for an approaching ball—the point in its flight which will give you the maximum chance of controlling your shot. Even though the push shots are hit without much spin or speed, correct timing is still necessary. The ideal contact point for the push is just *after* the ball has reached the top of its bounce. The ball must be hit as it starts its descent. As you make your backswing, try to visualize the entire swing in advance so that when you strike the approaching ball it will be *falling* onto your forward-moving racket.

From Figure 5*c*, the full backswing position, the stroke proceeds into the forward swing. There is no pause. In one fluidly rhythmical and continuous motion the bat is pushed forward into the path of the oncoming ball. The racket moves horizontally, the face of the bat still open, and once again the bat, wrist, and forearm move as one unit from the elbow. The head of the racket remains up and you still have the curve at the wrist. The elbow, having stayed close to its original point in the ready position, is now well in advance of the body (Figure 5*d*).

Figure 5

The backhand half volley

Even though the wrist and forearm are being moved, as I say, in one piece, I do not mean that there should be rigidity in the swing. The wrist is firm but not locked as though in a cast. The upper arm should be more relaxed but not so slack that it flops around.

Figure 5*e* shows that the horizontal path of the swing has continued until contact is made. At this crucial moment of the swing you must resist the overwhelming desire to slap, tap, jerk, or swat that poor little ball. Perhaps it is fear, perhaps it is improper timing, or perhaps it is the desire to score the point, that so often causes beginners to do these things. If your backswing has been properly synchronized to the ball's flight—that is, taken back in tempo with the ball—there should be no reason to apply this hasty, last-second jerk. Remember, this shot is called a push. Make it a push by trying to "hold" the ball on the racket as you hit it. Feel as though you are carrying it, caressing it. When properly executed, the moment of impact will barely be felt and the contact will seem like an accident that occurs midway between the backswing and the follow-through.

Never try to score the point using a push.

Note in Figure 5f, the contact point, that there is still the curve in the wrist and the racket head is up.

Figure 5g shows the position midway through the follow-through. The forearm, like a pendulum, continues to move forward from the elbow; the racket face is still open.

Figure 5h shows the full follow-through position. The forearm has been fully extended and now, along with the upper arm, points directly toward the net. The racket head is still up. It has struck the bottom surface of the ball with its slightly open, backward angle and it maintains that angle throughout the swing.

Practice this shot with an opponent or buddy who will feed balls to you right down the center of the table. He may also execute the shot at the same time. I must emphasize again that in learning the backhand push as I have described it you are not merely learning to return the ball just for the sake of getting it over the net. You are cultivating the beginnings of your backhand defense, so don't compromise. Take the backswing and the full follow-through that I have described, even though in so doing you miss the ball. The miss probably will be the result of poor timing, not of poor stroking. Your timing will improve with practice, but repeating a poor stroke until it becomes a habit, even though it gets the ball over the net at this early stage, will cause nothing but frustration later on.

Aside from the desire to jerk or tap the ball at the moment of impact, the only other difficulty in this shot will be the tendency of the ball, when struck with the racket face tilted back, to go higher than you want it to. With the backward angle of the racket you will strike the ball just below its center. The effect, of course, is that the ball will carry backspin and be somewhat lofted. The loft is merely a question of aim that practice will take care of. The backspin, at this stage, should not be deliberately applied by trying to rub the ball at the moment of impact. Later on, for the chopping shots, you will learn how to apply backspin by moving the wrist. Here the wrist stays in its original position.

It seems appropriate here to add a few general remarks about practice. You are, after all, learning a stroke through illustrations. Before you even begin to practice hitting the ball try to get your motion to coincide with the illustrations by practicing your stroke in the air, pausing during the backswing and at the follow-through to see that you are following the diagrams. Practice the motion slowly and try to analyze the path of the racket at every stage of the swing. Only when the motion becomes somewhat automatic (this should take about half an hour) should you attempt to return a ball with the stroke. This, of course is the big test. I can't tell you how often in private lessons I have seen my pupil execute a perfect stroke through the kind, static air only to have the stroke turn into a grotesque monster in the supercharged atmosphere that develops when the little white ball approaches.

Amateurs in any sport which requires hitting a ball—golf, tennis, even billiards—invariably ask at some point, "I don't see why the follow-through is so important. After all, nothing I do after I've struck the ball can affect it." "True enough," answers the expert, "but here is the point. The path your racket takes after you hit the ball is an extension of the path it has already taken in approaching the ball. A proper stroke, therefore, should carry the racket into the proper follow-through position because the definition of a proper stroke includes the follow-through."

To achieve steadiness and to cultivate the proper form for the backhand push, the ball should be hit back and forth at a constant rhythm. After you have gained some steadiness you can practice control by varying the rhythm—hitting the ball slightly higher and slower, or lower and faster.

The ideal steady push shot clears the net by about four inches and crosses it, between two experts, about 60 times a minute.

The Forehand Half Volley

The forehand half volley, or push, serves the same function as the backhand half volley—that is, it is a close-to-the-table defensive shot, except of course that it is used to return balls that are hit toward your right side, your forehand side. Once again it is a miniature of the longer-range forehand chop that you will need to return harder-hit balls. Unlike the backhand half volley, however, the forehand push requires some pivoting of the body for its proper execution and the stroke itself is somewhat longer. For these reasons it is more difficult to learn and should not be attempted until the pupil has some degree of ball control through practice of the backhand push described under "The Backhand Half Volley," which begins on page 36.

Here are the elements of the forehand push:

Let us assume that your opponent is serving and that you are standing in the same ready position as shown in Figure 5a. From this position you are prepared to shift toward your left for your backhand or toward your right for a forehand. Your opponent now serves forehand and angles the ball cross-court toward your right side. The serve is of moderate speed and depth and will clear the net by four inches or so. Without having as yet a forehand attacking stroke at your command the forehand push is called for.

As in the backhand push (and, indeed, as in all the other strokes in the game), your first reaction must be to gauge the speed and direction of the ball and enter into its rhythm by means of your backswing. Remember, the backswing is part of the entire stroke. There must be no pause, hesitation, or hitch at the top of the backswing. It flows into the forward action of the swing in a continuous movement.

(Make a quick check of your ready position once again. Your elbow is close to your right hip. The bat is well into the hand and your grip is firm and proper. Shake the bat like a hammer a few times to remind yourself that the control is from the hand. The bat is *not* an extension of your forearm. You must have a backward curve in the wrist.)

Figure 6a shows the initiation of the backswing for the forehand half volley. The first thing you feel as you draw your racket back is that the top edge of the head of your racket is moving back *first*. One of the most important features of this shot is that the elbow must be kept in front of the body close to the right hip and as near as possible to its original place in the ready position. It is the forearm that is moving back, not the elbow, and this is done by swiveling the forearm back in the elbow socket and by a pivot of the torso from left to right. It is this combination of the backward movement of the forearm and the pivot that gives the correct stroke.

It is essential to have some basic understanding of the pivot, for this is the only satisfactory method of transferring the weight evenly and smoothly throughout the swing. Visualize the pivot, as in golf, as revolving around the head. This means that while your neck and head remain relatively in place your shoulders, hips and torso are twisting around that focal point. Table-tennis players, just as do golfers, often develop into lungers. That is, on his backswing, instead of a proper pivot, the player throws his entire weight onto his rear foot without any simultaneous turning of the shoulders. This, of course, means that he is tilted backward, possibly with his left toe barely touching the floor, and all that is left to him now is to lunge into the ball or, at best, rock into it with a pushing motion rather than a swing.

Figure 6*b* shows the continuation of the backswing for the forehand half volley. The face of the bat has been opened during the swing to a 45-degree angle preparatory to striking toward the ball's bottom surface. The shoulders and upper torso have turned toward the right and the elbow is still close to the body and the top edge of the bat is still going back first. Note the curve in the wrist.

Figure 6*c* shows the top of the backswing. Your head is cocked slightly as the left eye sights the oncoming ball. During the pivot the knees have bent a bit more and the body "sits down" somewhat on the shot. The left hand is, of course, high for balance. The right elbow is still close to the body, for it has not been drawn back with the forearm. In this position, the top of the backswing, the forearm should be pointed out from the body at about "three o'clock" position. Throughout the backswing the wrist has gradually cocked the head of the bat so that now a line extended from the top edge of the bat through the handle would point toward the left-hand net post. In other words, though the forearm is at three o'clock the head of the bat is at five o'clock. At this point in your swing the ball is already on your side of the table and has probably just reached the top of its bounce. Now your stroke takes you toward the contact point.

Figure 6*d* shows the initiation of the forward swing. Now the bottom edge of the bat goes first. At this action on the forward

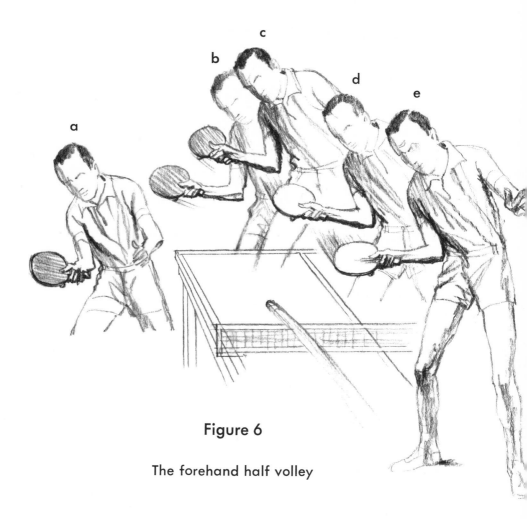

Figure 6

The forehand half volley

swing, there is no feeling that you are swinging the bat, the forearm or the wrist into the ball. The action is begun, rather, as an unpivoting of the torso. The forearm, wrist, and bat are moving into the ball as one unit only because the shoulders, now moving into the ball from left to right, are carrying them along. The swing effect will develop later in the stroke.

Figure 6e shows the forward swing somewhat farther along. The motion has been, so far, merely a reverse of the backswing, an unwinding. But now, just before contact, the forearm enters the action and begins to add a forward motion of its own by swiveling forward from the elbow. As the forearm enters the swing, the wrist, too, must catch up, and so, just before impact, the wrist moves the head of the bat into the ball. This wrist action is firm but without snap. The path of the forearm has been, and continues to be, almost horizontal, even though the bat is being taken toward the bottom surface of the ball.

Figure 6*f* shows the contact. The handle of the bat is parallel to the rear table edge; the wrist has turned the head of the bat into the ball so that the blade has been put against it square to the intended line of the ball's flight. Note too, in this illustration, that the upper arm, from shoulder to elbow, is angled forward pointing toward the table, not pointed vertically toward the floor. This

forward position of the elbow is maintained throughout the entire swing, for it is the elbow that serves as a hinge for the forearm to swing upon.

Figure 6g shows the stroke midway through the follow-through. The ball has been struck on its bottom surface with the bat tilted back in its original open angle. There has been no jerking or swatting with the wrist at the moment of impact. Steadiness is the object here, not power, and the swing has been contained and controlled. At this point in the follow-through the forearm is continuing the motion it developed before the contact and is moving faster than the pivot of the body. Therefore it is separating from the upper part of the arm, like scissors that are being swung open. (Note Figure 6c showing the top of the backswing. Forearm and upper arm are close together in a narrow V, the closed scissors.)

Figure 6h shows the full follow-through position. This illustration is of course a crucial checkpoint in determining whether the stroke has been correctly executed or not. The correct follow-through position cannot be reached if there have been errors along the way. First, note the crucial fact that now, in the follow-through, the wrist, forearm, and upper arm are all in a straight line. The forearm has been entirely "let out" and there is no longer a bend at the elbow. The wrist, too, has moved through the ball so that the head of the racket is also in line with the forearm and upper arm. To be certain that you have let the wrist go through the shot make sure that the thumb is on a straight line with the arm, not pointed to the right of it. The blade of the bat is still open.

Learning the table game correctly—that is, the forehand and backhand half volley—will greatly increase the speed with which the player develops the other strokes of the game, for the essentials of all the strokes are contained in these elementary push shots. It might be well, therefore, to point out a number of common errors that seem to arise in the learning process.

The most frequent errors are those resulting from poor timing: jerking at the moment of impact, failure to take a backswing or follow-through, or hitting the ball too soon or too late. Timing is a phase of the game that is very difficult to teach, either in private lessons or through words in a book. Some people seem to have a built-in timer or, as I prefer to call it, a "sense of ball." Others seem to flail helplessly at every shot. An expert with good form can handle a ball traveling toward him at 120 m.p.h. and make it seem as though he were playing in slow motion; another player, sometimes even quite advanced, will give the impression that his strokes, even the simple half volleys, are epileptic seizures.

Though timing is difficult to teach, here are a few guidelines that the player seeking to improve his game may refer to.

First of all, on every stroke, timing begins with the ready position. An alert anticipatory position allows you that extra split second in which to gauge the ball's speed, direction, and trajectory, and to enter into its rhythm as you take your backswing. If poor anticipation forces you to hurry your backswing or, worse, to abandon it, no proper stroke can be expected. All of the world's great players draw their rackets back *as* the ball approaches and, while the game's champions have fine built-in clocks, a good guide for beginners or intermediate players is to have the tempo of their backswing coincide with the tempo of the ball as it approaches.

Another aspect of timing that can be learned to some extent is to judge the ideal point of contact on the ball's trajectory. Often I see players executing their half-volley shots (and their drives) by hitting the ball just at the top of its bounce. Apparently the notion is that if the ball is hit at its zenith there will be more room to clear the net. Actually, hitting the ball at the top of its bounce is too difficult to make this extra clearance space worthwhile. The ball must be intercepted after it has decelerated and begun its descent. So, another crucial checkpoint for the player should be that he is striking the ball just after it begins to drop. On the half-volley shots he should have the feeling that the ball is *falling* onto his inward-moving racket—falling into a "pocket." Though you are taking the ball lower you can still clear the net easily by merely increasing the backward angle of your bat—that is, by opening the face of it to allow more loft.

Aside from poor timing, there are other errors to be avoided on the half volley.

Scooping the ball during the shot. This means simply that the player allows the path of his racket to describe a curve during the stroke, apparently with the idea of getting more underneath the ball, either to increase the spin by rubbing the ball, or to increase control by cradling the ball. This scooping or cradling motion may seem smooth and fluid and may even appear to give the stroke some eye appeal but it is fundamentally wrong, as it does not take the racket through the ball cleanly enough. Taking the racket through cleanly is necessary in the more potent chop shots that you will later learn, for there the object is to apply spin, and it is the speed of the racket grazing the ball's lower surface that does this. Scooping is therefore antitheoretical. To avoid scooping or cradling, try to imagine that on the backswing the top edge of your bat is going back through a narrow alley just wide enough for the bat to slide in provided it stays in the same plane. If you roll your wrist to scoop or cradle the ball you will be taking the bat out of that narrow alley and it will scrape the walls. On the forward part of the swing the lower edge of the blade goes first, again sliding exactly in that alley it traversed for the backswing.

Failure to "let out" the forearm and wrist on the follow-through. Though this common error is often the result of poor timing it sometimes is the result of fear. The idea seems to be that by holding back, checking the swing, the player will have more control. Check the follow-through positions for the forehand and backhand push shots and make sure that your follow-through position corresponds to them. The racket must reach that position regardless of what happens to the ball. Timing can be improved through practice, but relearning a poor stroke that has been grooved into a habit is almost impossible. Follow through!

Trying to score points with the half volley. This is another common error. The backhand and forehand push shots are passive, defensive strokes. A champion will never try to force his opponent into an error by using an extra-hard push. The most you can hope for with the push is to keep the ball reasonably low and away from your opponent's strong point. To learn the pushing strokes you should play them metronomically down the middle of the table. Only later, after you have developed the strokes and some ball control, should you attempt to move the ball around the table; even then the half volleys are never played near the outer white lines.

As you learn the half-volley shots, experiment with different blade angles to vary the trajectory of the ball; opening the blade will get the ball higher and closing it will keep the ball lower. But don't get the idea that this is the only way of controlling the height of the ball. Later on, for the more aggressive defensive chops, you will see that even with a perfectly flat blade, one that is face up like a saucer, you can still keep the ball skimming over the net.

Footwork

Up to now we have considered only the two most elementary shots in the game, the forehand and backhand half volley, and even in these it was assumed that the ball had been hit directly toward you. This was merely a convenience to enable you to concentrate on the stroke without having to worry about the additional aspect of footwork. In actual play, footwork is indissolubly united with the strokes, for almost never does a ball fall into that "pocket" I spoke of without the help of your feet.

Footwork, like timing, is quite difficult to learn. At its best it comes naturally and there is as much grace in the movements of table tennis as there is in tennis or track, or ballet. Indeed, an exuberant sportswriter once described me as a "flashing dancing master." Though footwork cannot be taught, some fundamentals can be set down so that players learning the game can have at least some idea of what they should be doing. In private teaching I rarely attempt to impose upon a pupil a rigid model of footwork since it is most difficult to alter what seems to be an instinctive or natural movement. Even among the game's great masters, who conform quite closely to basic principles when executing the strokes, there is a great diversity of footwork.

One thing is certain, however: the better your footwork, the better you will play the sport. Try to think of it this way. The various strokes you learn are, ideally, made in exactly the same way on every shot. If, for example, you learn the proper stroke, timing, and follow-through for the forehand drive you will want to execute these fundamentals correctly on every forehand attacking shot you attempt. But this can be done only if your legs put you into the same relative position to the ball for each new return. Insofar as your legs fail to put you into place you will have to make instantaneous corrections of the stroke or timing by stretching or flailing. Your legs are like bicycle wheels that roll you into position so that your arm can do its work. When your legs are taking you into position, every shot will look easy and your game will appear effortless and graceful.

When I think of great footwork in an athlete, somehow I always remember the way Joe DiMaggio played center field. I rarely remember his making a difficult catch. There existed a kind of oneness between him and the ball so that every batter seemed to hit the ball at just the right height and speed so that it plopped into

DiMaggio's waiting glove. Inherent in this seeming effortlessness, of course, is something that is called "anticipation"—the ability to move in the direction that the ball will be hit before it is actually hit. In table tennis this comes through experience and the cultivation of the habit of watching the ball and being conscious of your opponent's movements at the same time. But for the present let's consider some examples of elementary footwork involved in executing the forehand and backhand half volley—footwork that is essentially the same as you will later use to return the hardest kill shots.

Just for a minute glance back at Figure 5a, the ready position for the return of service. Let us assume now that your opponent's service, instead of being hit directly toward you, has been hit from his forehand court straight down the sideline toward your backhand. The ball is traveling at medium speed so that its ideal interception point requires only that you move toward your left without having to retreat or come forward. You can, of course, remain in your ready position stance and attempt to execute your backhand half volley from there but, unless you are wearing diver's shoes, that is the hard way. A six-inch step to your left with your left foot should put you into perfect position.

As the ball approaches, you move out of the ready position by stepping to the left. Your weight will fall onto your left foot as you move and the left knee will bend a bit more to cushion the shock. As the step is being taken, your racket is being drawn back toward your waist as the backswing for the half volley. If you have judged your step correctly, the ball is now headed right toward your midsection and you are prepared to execute the perfectly timed push.

Note: It is absolutely crucial to keep the left hand up, wrist higher than elbow, throughout this movement. As soon as your left hand drops, it will put you as much out of balance as if you were carrying a suitcase full of rocks in your left hand.

Here is another example of the footwork for the backhand push. The ball has now been served from your opponent's backhand corner and is traveling at a sharp angle toward your backhand side. Also, it has been served somewhat short so that in addition to the movement of your body from right to left, you must get in closer as well to intercept the ball at the proper contact point. Now all the elements of backhand defensive play come into use.

The ball has been angled sharply to you from corner to corner.

Your step must be wide enough so that at contact you will not have to reach with your arm and change your stroke. One wide step may accomplish this but this is apt to leave you awkwardly straddling a lot of floor space. It is simpler to make a short step with your right foot by way of preparation and then a somewhat longer forward and leftward step with your left foot which, if done properly, should leave you in relatively the same position as you were for the previous example—that is, with the ball headed for that pocket you have prepared for it.

Another example, somewhat more difficult: The ball has been served from your opponent's backhand court to your backhand court, but this time the serve has been made higher and deeper. On a shot of this type your first consideration must be to keep the ideal contact point in *front* of you. You must not allow the ball to get behind you. *You* must get behind *it*. To do this you will shift your left foot to the rear as you take your backswing. Along with this shifting backward and to the left there is the leaning of the weight onto the left side. The reason for this backward step, of course, is that you can take the ball as it descends. If you were to remain in the ready position two feet behind the table, this high bouncing ball would still be rising as it reached you. This retreat, therefore, onto the left foot for the backhand (and the right foot for the forehand) is really the beginning of defensive play.

The examples I have given above for the elementary footwork involved in making the backhand half volley hold true also for the forehand half volley, except of course that you must step toward the ball with the right foot for that shot.

The only other remarks to make concerning footwork at this point are that you should try to cultivate the habit of an alert ready position that will enable you to step toward the ball on either side as soon as it leaves your opponent's bat—or even sooner if you can anticipate the direction.

Get into the habit, too, of taking short, quick steps, rather than long, lazy ones. Tall players with long arms and legs often fall victim to this bad habit of striding with giant steps toward the ball. This usually puts them into poor position and they compound this habit of poor footwork by another bad habit—they tend to rely on their long reach to extricate themselves from a poor last-minute position. Thus their strokes are less grooved than are those of shorter players who must get on their bicycles to get to the ball on every shot. Hungary's Ferenc Sido and England's Johnny Leach, both over six feet and both former world champions, are beautiful exceptions to the generalizations I have made above.

The Block Shot

Before concluding this section of the book dealing with the table game, there is one more simple shot over which you should have some command: the block. It may be that you already have some idea of it, as it is the kind of shot used by players without any formal knowledge of the strokes. Before I ever set foot in my first table-tennis club I was quite a competent "blocker" through my games at home over the dining-room table.

Though there is really no such shot as a forehand block, on the backhand side the block is now a vital shot. I say "now" because in the days when the game was played with normal pimpled-rubber rackets the backhand block was used only rarely by experts on those occasions when they were trapped close to the table and saw a hard-hit drive coming at them with no time for retreat. The modern-day game with sponge rackets is so much faster, however, that the block shot on the backhand is commonly used either as a defensive shot when trapped close to the table, or as a means of sustaining the attack by returning the ball quickly against an opponent who is eager to take the attack away from you.

The essence of the block shot is simplicity. Ideally, the bat is merely placed in the path of the oncoming ball and the ball's own velocity bounces it back across the net without the player applying any additional forward motion with his bat. The block shot can be used during a rally or on a return of service that is faster than one anticipated, but in either case it must be used only in answer to a ball that carries sufficient velocity to make the rebound possible without additional help. In a sense, the block is a compromise between defense and attack and it should never be used if either a full attacking stroke or a full defensive stroke is possible.

Figure 7 shows the position just after contact for the block shot. Answering a quick serve or drive to his backhand (or being trapped at the table) the player tilts his racket downward toward the table, closing its face, and intercepts the oncoming ball. With this racket angle he can return the hard-hit topspinned ball and still keep it low

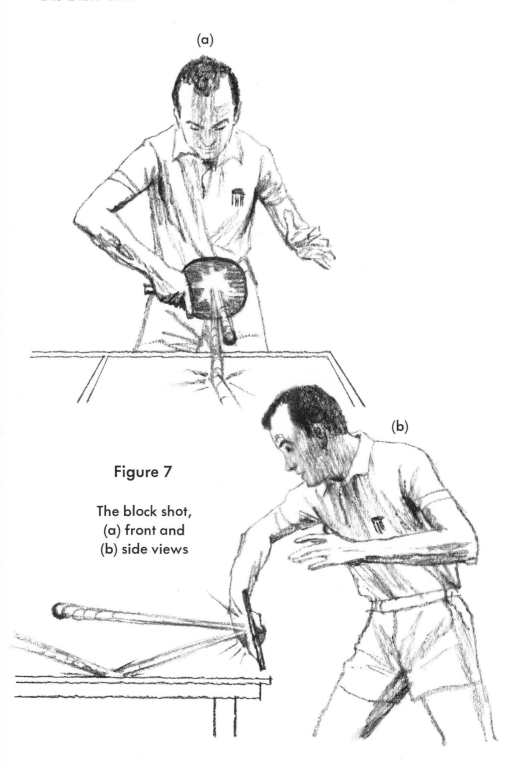

(a)

(b)

Figure 7

The block shot,
(a) front and
(b) side views

over the net. Also, by not adding any forward motion as he contacts the ball, he will absorb some of its speed.

Unlike the half volley, the block shot is made by contacting the ball while it is on the rise, before the top of the bounce. In a sense, this is a pickup, for the bat is almost touching the table as it waits for the ball.

Only practice against fast services will give the ˙player the "touch" for the block by allowing him to experiment with different downward angles of the bat for different speed balls. You will, no doubt, find that to absorb the shock of a really fast shot just by placing the bat in front of the ball and allowing it to rebound is not good enough. The ball may have sufficient speed or topspin to cause your return to fly over the table end notwithstanding the fact that you kept your bat stationary at the moment of impact. On such shots you will have to compensate for the speed and/or spin by actually drawing your racket back from the ball just before the moment of impact. This means that just before impact the bat is actually traveling backward toward your body, in the same direction as the ball. This is accomplished by a tiny movement of the hand only, and it takes the bat back just a few inches but this is enough to keep the ball on the table.

If you are working with the buddy system I recommended at the beginning of this book, a good way to practice the block is to have your buddy serve fast topspins aimed directly at your body. Anticipating these, you should crowd the table a bit and let the ball bounce right into your midsection where your waiting racket will block it back.

Note: Do not try to absorb the speed of a shot by loosening your grip on the bat. True, by loosening your grip you make the bat less rigid and it will absorb more speed. But you will also sacrifice control and be led into errors. The bat must be held firmly in the hand at all times, particularly at the moment of impact. To absorb a very fast shot with the block, use the little backward motion I suggested.

Since a forehand block is extremely awkward to execute, you will always have to choose between attack and defense when playing a ball hit to your forehand.

Second Solo Exercise

The forehand and backhand half volley and the block are the elementary but essential strokes of the game. I can't think of a better way to make rapid progress in learning the sport than to practice the table game diligently. Even after I had won a handful of U. S. titles I invariably set aside a half hour of every practice session before a major tournament for just pushing the ball back and forth with half volleys to sensitize my touch.

Aside from practicing the table game against other players I developed a method of using a wall as a backboard, and for the most rapid development of your game I suggest that you spend a half hour of your practice sessions this way. Take the net off your table-tennis table and slide the entire table lengthwise against a wall. If the table can be unbolted at the center without difficulty, one half of the table will do even better. The idea of this exercise is to hit your forehand and backhand half volley into the wall as many times as possible without missing.

You start off by merely tossing the ball upward a bit with your left hand and letting it bounce on the table in front of you. Start with the backhand push first, using the stroke I have illustrated. The slight backspin you engender because of the backward tilt of the racket will cause the ball to fall more vertically off the wall than it otherwise would do, and thus, if properly controlled, it will keep dropping back onto the table. As it returns to you from the wall it will be carrying topspin, a spin rotating toward you, just as it would from the bat of an opponent who has given you a medium-speed attacking shot to handle.

Remember that the same form must be used when practicing against the wall as was illustrated for the half-volley strokes. Keep your left hand up, take your backswing toward the pit of the stomach (for the backhand), carry the ball forward with the pushing motion, and follow through so that your forearm has extended itself as far as it will go in the forward direction through the path of the ball. The only deviation you should make is that when hitting against the wall your target area is higher than the half volley over a net. Make your target area about twenty inches above the edge of the table against the wall. Too low a target will cause the ball to rebound too rapidly to maintain control. Thus, with a higher target, instead of making the path of your racket horizontal, you must incline it upward as you stroke into the ball.

Do not hit the ball too hard. What you are striving for is steadiness and control. Try to make your rhythm constant in this exercise —metronomic. If you have reached a stage of control in the first exercise I recommended that permits you to tap up fifty successive balls in good rhythm, you should be able to play twenty-five consecutive half volleys against the wall fairly easily. When you have reached this goal of twenty-five shots with the backhand, switch over to the forehand push and try to reach twenty-five shots with that stroke. Then vary your shots, backhand and forehand with an occasional block shot thrown in. Bear in mind in this exercise that every time you deviate from the rhythm you are trying to maintain you have made an error. While this error may appear of minor importance when you are practicing against a wall—it has forced you to hurry your next shot a bit to recover the rhythm or it has sent the ball a bit higher or lower than you intended—it actually is a gross error that during a match would have cost you a point.

Note: Do not intersperse more than an occasional block shot. The block is a necessary tool but it leads nowhere. Concentrate on the half volley. Its long follow-through and the backward angle of the bat at contact will be preparing you for long-range defensive play fifteen feet behind the table.

Also, do not worry about the twenty-inch-high target area I suggested. It is not too high. True, the net is only *six* inches above the table, but by developing ball control you will be able to transfer your shot to any height you want later on.

If you do not own a table-tennis table, any table thirty inches high (most tables are) will do for this exercise. If it is a narrow table, pull it out a foot or two from the wall.

This section of the book dealing with the table game is more or less completed. You now have in your repertoire three basic strokes (the forehand and backhand half volley and the block) and you have two exercises to practice as well. This is enough to keep a man busy for quite a while. I recommend that you spend at least twenty hours practicing the push shots and exercises before proceeding to the next section. Try to quell the appetite that urges you to "hurry up and play, hurry up and play." While the preceding chapters offer, I admit, a somewhat bland diet, the food is nourishing and vital to proper development. Moreover, it should be digested slowly. Go over the illustrations once again, forgetting about the ball. Concentrate only on getting the proper stroke grooved, even if you can make it only in the air. Remember, one of your goals is to look like a champion even if you can't play like one. If this mimicry is made a goal in itself, surprisingly enough there usually follows an improvement in actual play. There are no champions with poor strokes.

Once you understand that even the most elementary shot in table tennis must be "stroked" you have come a long way. A return is never so simple that it is merely tapped back across the net. Timing, footwork, and bodywork right down to the use of the left hand for balance are constituents of every shot no matter how easy it may appear.

CHAPTER 4

The Attack: The Forehand Drive

As I have already emphasized, all shots in table tennis must be controlled with spin. On the attack, the extreme power with which the ball is hit lessens the safety margin so that the proper control of topspin—the spin that keeps a hard-hit ball from flying off the table end—is vital. Topspin, a spin that rotates the ball toward your opponent, forces the light, fast-moving ball to dip downward as it crosses the net just as a baseball pitcher delivers a "sinker" by spinning the baseball toward the batter. In table tennis, even the kill of a high setup is made with topspin.

As I have already pointed out in the chapter on the grip, the Orientals are the world's best forehand attacking players. This is due primarily, in my opinion, to their use of the penholder grip. To reinforce my argument I should say that most often, wherever an Oriental player has appeared in international play using the shakehands grip, he has been a defensive player, not an attacker. Why the penholder grip should be so suited for the forehand attack will become clear as we proceed.

On the attack, the object, of course, is to hit the ball so hard that your opponent cannot return it. At the same time topspin must be applied to make the ball drop as it crosses the net. So, actually, two motions are involved:

1. A forward motion of the racket into the ball for power.

2. An upward motion of the racket which applies the spin as the gripping surface of the blade contacts the top rear surface of the ball.

Figure 8 shows the forehand drive of three-time world champion, Chuang Tse-tung.

Figure 8

The forehand drive with penholder grip as
shown by three-time world champion
Chuang Tse-tung

There are two particular points I would like you to note in this drawing, for they illustrate what I consider to be the crucial elements of correct attacking play made with *either* the penholder grip *or* the shakehands grip.

First, note that as the racket is brought toward the ball the racket head is pointed *down*. The handle is pointed up.

Second, note that the face of the blade is cocked back and held almost at a right angle to the forearm. In other words, the bat is *not* used as an extension of the forearm.

The reason these two points are crucial is that they allow the most potent and economical production of the motions needed on the drive; the upward motion for spin, and the inward motion for power. Here is how they are applied:

1. The downward position of the head of the bat—a six o'clock position, let's call it—allows the player as he approaches the ball to turn the head of the bat upward with his wrist in a semicircle until on the follow-through it reaches a twelve o'clock position. It is this upward circular action of the head of the bat that should apply the spin. One of the most common faults in the strokes of players using the shakehands grip is that they approach the ball on the forehand drive with the racket head *already up,* and thereby lose the additional acceleration of the racket head that the penholder players achieve because they are forced by their grip to approach the ball with the head of the bat down.

2. Just as the racket must move upward over the back surface of the ball to apply spin, it must, at the same time, move forward into the ball to apply power. Therefore, if the ball is approached with the racket head *already forward,* as it is when a player uses the racket as an extension of his forearm, once again the additional acceleration achieved by the penholder players—whose grip automatically forces them to cock the head of the bat—is lost.

Figure 9 shows a shakehands player approaching the ball and committing the two most common errors that account for unsuccessful attacking strokes: (1) the head of the bat is already up, reducing the amount of topspin he can apply; and (2) the head of the bat is already forward on a straight line with the forearm, reducing the power he can obtain during the swing.

Bear in mind these two crucial points as I now illustrate what I consider to be the ideal stroking method for the forehand drive made with the shakehands grip. I shall describe two types of fore-

Figure 9

Incorrect approach for the forehand
drive, using the shakehands grip

hand strokes: the European-type forehand drive whose best exponents were the world champions Ferenc Sido of Hungary and Bohumil Vana of Czechoslovakia, and my own forehand stroke, sometimes called by exuberant analysts the "Miles forehand."

The European Forehand Attack

Figure 10*a* shows the ready position. On the forehand attack the stroke must be made with the left shoulder toward the net. It is a sideways stance as in golf. Thus the ready position here, anticipating an attacking opportunity, is already somewhat shifted toward the right.

Figure 10*b* shows only three differences from the ready position: (*a*) the wrist has already begun to drop so that it points the head of the bat downward; (*b*) the wrist has already begun to cock backward so that it will later be able to release the head of the bat into the ball for power; (*c*) the weight has begun to shift toward the right foot, leaving the left foot free to step into the ball as it approaches.

Figure 10*c* shows the natural continuation of the backswing. The wrist has continued its descent and has cocked even more. The body has continued its pivot from left to right. Notice that the elbow, still bent, is held close to the body. This rhythmical backswing is, of course, the essential element in correct timing. From the moment the ball leaves your opponent's racket you must enter into its rhythm and anticipate the ideal contact point for it. Your backswing sets the tempo.

Figure 10*d* shows the continuation of the pivot and the shifting of the left foot, toe first, toward the oncoming ball. The arm has extended farther, but the elbow is still close to the body.

Figure 10*e* shows the full backswing position. The arm is straighter (but not rigid) and the player is drawing a left-eyed bead on the ball over his shoulder. The wrist is fully cocked and the head of the bat is *down*. The left hand is held high to maintain the balance.

This is the ideal backswing position for the forehand drive made in the European manner. When this position is reached, the ball should be approaching its contact point and the racket should be down well below that point. From here the racket will be swung upward in an underhand stroke, much like the stroke used in bowling, until it ends in a follow-through behind the *right* ear. Note that the racket does not cross the body from right to left as it does in lawn tennis. The swing ends behind the right ear.

Now for the forward swing.

There is no pause between the top of the backswing and the start of the forward swing. Note that in Figures 10*e* and 10*f* the relative positions of the arm, wrist, and bat are much the same. Even though they have begun to move forward into the ball neither the arm nor the wrist is responsible for that movement. It is the body, rather, uncoiling from its pivot with a twisting of the hips and shoulders to the left, that is *dragging* the upper arm, forearm, and wrist and bat toward the ball. Later in the swing, in the final phase before impact, the forearm will accelerate to catch up with the unpivoting and, just before impact, the wrist will enter the action, in turn catching up with the forearm and adding the final impetus for power. But in Figure 10*f* notice that the head of the bat is still pointed down and is still cocked back.

Figure 10*g* shows the final phase before impact. Here, for the purposes of instruction, we have imagined the ball to be already waiting at its ideal contact point. It has descended from the top of its bounce (on a defensive underspinned return from our opponent) and is *falling* onto our forward and upward moving racket. At this point on the swing the forearm is accelerating, taking the bat upward toward the ball by swiveling in the elbow socket. The wrist is just about ready to turn the racket head upward to apply the spin and at the same time move smartly forward from its cocked position to deliver the power by accelerating the racket head into the ball. The wrist is a hinge that moves in and up at the same time.

Figure 10*g* is extremely important, for this is the crucial moment in the swing. Careful analysis is important. All of your footwork, body motion, and arm motion have, up to here, been timed so that at this moment of the swing the ball will be at that part of the bounce which you pre-visualized as the ideal contact point and your racket will be ready to deliver the maximum power coupled with the spin necessary to keep the ball on the table.

When I talk of maximum power, incidentally, I do not mean that every attacking shot is hit as hard as possible. What I mean, rather, is maximum speed of the ball for the power expended. The swing must deliver power *economically*. The more economical the effort in delivering power, the more ease and efficiency of the swing

Figure 10

The European forehand drive

even on the easy shots, the more will be your control over the explosive smashes you will eventually learn to hit.

Figure 10h shows the moment of contact. This is the moment of power. The forearm is still accelerating but now, in addition, the wrist has entered the shot by moving the racket head briskly upward and inward toward the ball.

On the upward movement that applies the spin try to get the feeling that as you turn the head of the bat up onto the ball you are brushing the ball off your racket. You should definitely not have the feeling that you are trying to prolong the moment of contact by *rubbing* the ball. The spin is applied not so much by the racket's grippiness as by the speed of the bat as it grazes the ball.

For the power, the forward movement of the wrist must be brisk but not wild. It should be in the nature of a tightly controlled slap. The harder you wish to hit the ball, the faster the racket head must be snapped into the ball. But no matter how hard you hit, the racket head is never snapped so much into the ball that it either breaks over beyond the line of the forearm or even lines up parallel with it. In other words, throughout the stroke, the wrist maintains some of its backward angle relative to the forearm.

Note that in Figure 10h, the moment of impact, the face of the racket is square to the intended line of the ball's flight. The ball that we have chosen for this illustration is a medium ball whose best contact point is just a few inches above the net's height. The intended line of flight for it, if it is to be hit with some speed, is about straight out so that it clears the net by several inches. Even so, in the best type of forehand stroke, even the hardest-hit balls leave the racket in a slightly upward trajectory. It is the combination of gravity and topspin that forces the ball to fall as it crosses the table. The upward trajectory varies, of course, with the height of the ball as it bounces toward its contact point and the speed with which it is to be hit. The lower the bounce the more upward must the trajectory be to clear the net; a higher bounce allows more of a margin for error and the trajectory can be straighter toward the target. The test of a good stroke is whether it allows the player to take a low bouncing ball, one that just skims the net, and hit it on the table with full power.

Note, in Figure 10h, that the forearm and wrist have so completely taken over command of the shot that, rather than being dragged by the turning of the right shoulder, they are now well in advance of the right shoulder. From the time the wrist entered the swing, the head of the bat became the fastest moving part of the stroke.

Figure 10*i* shows the position just after contact. The wrist has ceased its forward movement at impact, but it is still moving upward, taking the head of the bat in a tight semicircle to its goal just behind the right ear. Note that the forearm, throughout the follow-through, stays bent at the elbow. This means that on the follow-through as the forearm goes back toward the right ear, the right elbow must be raised.

Figure 10*j* shows the position almost at the end of the follow-through. The body has continued its pivot. The chest has turned almost square to the line of flight and the weight has shifted to the left side by a turning on the ball of the right foot.

Figure 10*k* shows the follow-through completed. The bat is being snapped briskly into its pocket behind the right ear and the head of the bat has turned so much that the handle is parallel to the floor. There is still the backward curve of the wrist. The chest is square to the direction of the shot. There has been no slackening of the tension that was felt in the hand and wrist at the moment of impact. In other words, the follow-through must be firm. If, after the impact, the racket head is allowed to flop or whip around loosely, the shot, too, will be sloppy.

Figure 10*l* shows the bat descending back into the ready position in anticipation of the next shot. For beginners, particularly, it is important to cultivate this habit of returning to the ready position after completing the follow-through. Too often players learning the strokes become so intent on taking their racket into the proper follow-through position that they become immobilized when they reach it. As a result they begin their next shot by taking their backswing from that position with the racket behind their ear. This results in a mechanical, robotlike style that does not take into account the ever-changing rhythms of one's opponent. Ideally, every shot should begin from a ready position which is more or less neutral.

What I have just analyzed for you is the forehand drive made in the European style—that is, using the shakehands grip but incorporating into the stroke the main principles of the penholder grip. Since the forehand drive is probably the game's most important stroke I am going to analyze another variation of it so that

Figure 11

The "Miles" forehand drive

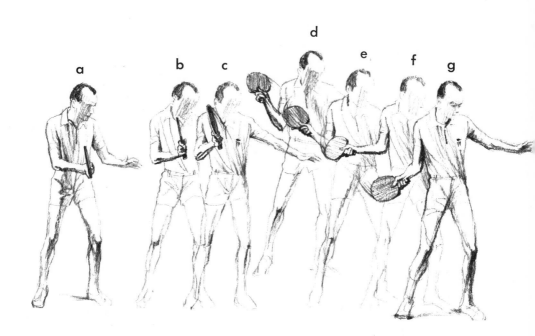

you may experiment and decide which one best suits your game. When I was playing my best game the international table-tennis world credited me with having the game's best forehand drive from the point of view of both consistency and power. Though my stroke seemed quite unique (although not unorthodox) to some experts, it came quite naturally to me. It was described variously as "rotary," "windmill," "circular," and "whiplash"—all stemming from the fact that I took a circular backswing preparatory to the forward swing. The main function of the backswing, of course, is to better time the ball and to gain momentum which will be converted into power at the moment of impact. But let's take a look at the stroke.

Figure 11*a* shows the ready position.

Figure 11*b* shows the beginning of the backswing, which in this stroke is initiated by a slight *upward* movement of the wrist which raises the racket head. In the European forehand, remember, the back swing immediately points the racket head *down*.

Figure 11*c* shows that the racket continues its upward path. The forearm, moving from the elbow, goes up and takes the blade close to the chin. Because the body is pivoting, the right elbow stays very close to the body on the backswing.

Figure 11*d* shows the racket at its maximum height in the circular backswing. The head of the bat still points up, but it is preparing to drop as the forearm descends.

In Figure 11*e* the racket head drops downward as the racket continues on the circle, now heading down. The forearm is still close to the body and forms a V with the upper arm.

In Figure 11*f* the forearm and racket head level off. The wrist has been cocked back. At this point—and this is quite a delicate element—the body, pivoting toward the left, begins to drag the forearm forward into the ball. The right shoulder, at this point moving faster than the forearm, is pulling away from the forearm so that the arm straightens out a little. The racket head has now continued on its circle and is moving down.

In Figure 11*g* the forward swing is now under way and the racket head is well below the intended contact point. From here on

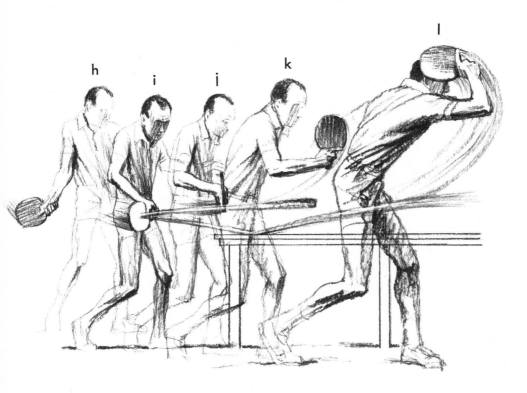

the stroke will be much the same as the European-type forehand.

Figure 11*h* shows the position just before contact. All the power that has been held in reserve by the cocked wrist is now turned on by accelerating the racket head inward and upward toward the ball. The backswing, by taking an upward path first, has increased this possible acceleration.

Figure 11*i* shows the moment of contact. The bat is level now—that is, the handle is horizontal. There is no feeling of hesitation as the ball is hit. The path of the racket was fixed after the ball had been timed by the backswing. The bat is headed for that pocket behind the right ear. Swing it there!

In *j, k,* and *l* of Figure 11 the follow-through is completed.

The attacking shots are not easily learned, either through a book or through private coaching. They are, to put it simply, hard to perfect. But what I have given you here are the basic stroking principles of the world's great attacking players. To be sure, all players, including champions, differ slightly in their swings, but the strokes of the champions all adhere closely to the fundamentals regardless of individual deviations. What I have set up, however, in the preceding analysis is a composite model on which to model your attack. The closer you adhere to the illustrations the surer you can be that you will not violate any fundamentals.

Here are a few suggestions for developing the attack:

Unfortunately, the method of using a wall, which is so useful for practicing the half volley and, as you will see, the defensive shots, will not do for the attack. The defensive shots carry underspin that forces the ball downward from the wall to the practice table just as they carry the ball downward off your opponent's bat. The attacking shots, on the other hand, carry topspin, and balls hit against a wall will overshoot the practice table. Therefore, you must have an opponent, preferably one who has learned to underspin a bit. In private lessons I always teach the defensive shots before the attack, but since you cannot execute a defensive shot except in answer to a ball hit with topspin, it seemed wise, for the purposes of this book, to discuss the attack first since that shot can be made against even a half volley. If you are using the buddy system to learn, one player can feed half volleys right down the center of the table to the player practicing the drive. Your first step is to groove the stroke in the air—very slowly at first. Choose either my forehand stroke or the European stroke and swing it in the air so often that you have the

Figure 12

The "Miles" forehand drive: a composite

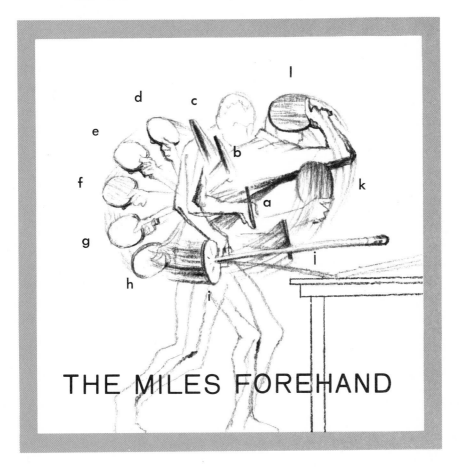

feeling it is part of you. Increase the tempo as you begin to "feel" the swing.

Your next step is your fight with the moving ball. The moving ball, of course, is what makes table tennis so difficult to master. Not only must you make the correct stroke but you must time it so that impact is made at precisely the correct fraction of a second. Imagine how difficult golf would be if the ball were pitched to the player instead of being hit while at rest.

The fight with the moving ball offers two obstacles. The first is getting your feet to take you to the ideal position for the swing. Frequently your feet will take you to the swinging zone too early or too late. Sometimes they will not take you to the swinging zone at all. If you can imagine a batter in baseball having to run up to home plate as the pitcher uncoiled you will have an idea of the precise timing table tennis requires. All I will say about footwork here is that if you begin practicing the attack quite slowly, always taking the ready position first and having the balls pushed softly toward your swinging zone, your footwork will develop quite naturally. I need only point out the obvious here that the left foot is the master foot in the attack. On the backswing when the weight shifts to the right foot, the left foot is free to step into the ball and place the body in the correct position.

The other difficulty that is created by the moving ball is the timing of the swing. Champions in the master class time the ball automatically and probably never had to learn or analyze. But beginners or intermediate players are often only hazily aware that something is wrong with their swing without being able to spot the trouble. Often it is the basic understanding of timing which is at fault—that is, at what point on the ball's flight it should be intercepted.

It would be a natural assumption that if the ball were contacted at the highest point of its trajectory there would be a greater margin of safety in clearing the net. In practice, however, this does not work. The best attacking players hit their attacking shots (against defensive returns) just as the ball starts to descend or, as we say, just off the top of the bounce. (Compare this, by the way, with the serve in lawn tennis, where the best service method is to hit the ball just off the top of the throw, not at the height of the throw.)

You should have the feeling when making attacking strokes that the ball itself is helping you apply spin by *falling* onto your upward-moving racket. It is the combination of these movements in opposite directions that actually helps you. When the ball is hit at the top of the bounce, or before, only the racket can put the spin on. Usually players who hit at the top of the bounce approach the ball with the racket head up and their tendency is to smother the ball by getting too much on top of it. These players always find the greatest difficulty in hitting heavy underspin and it is usually netted. If the ball is hit as it descends, as it should be, it is almost impossible to approach the ball with the racket head up. It must be kept down. Try it.

Note: Later, when I discuss the counter-drives—that is, attack against attack—you will see that you must often take the ball on the rise, here sacrificing the extra margin of safety you might gain by retreating (to allow the ball to fall) in order to gain the advantage of a quicker return from closer to the table.

Figure 13a shows the correct contact point for attacking shots made in answer to defensive returns. Line A–D represents the ball's trajectory. Point B is the top of the bounce. Point C is where the ball should be intercepted.

Even in killing high balls, I make my putaway shot by allowing the ball to fall just a bit from its height.

Figure 13

(a) The correct contact point for attacking shots answering defensive returns; (b) the putaway shot

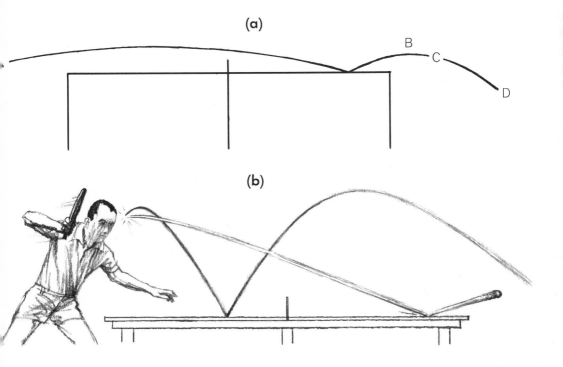

Figure 13*b* shows the bat approaching contact for a high putaway. Notice that here the stroke has changed by allowing the elbow to be raised. On high shots, this is the only change in the stroke, incidentally. The elbow, around which the forearm rotates, is raised and is no longer kept close to the body.

Aside from the errors accountable to the moving ball, there are others that frequently pop up. Here are some of the most common ones with some homemade remedies.

Turning the racket over on the ball. An underhand swing with an open racket that will hit the ball hard and still keep it on the table seems counter to what we should expect. Many beginners feel that they have to turn the top edge of the bat over on top of the ball to make the ball go toward the target over the net.

Figure 14 shows the racket just after contact trying this method. Avoid this at all costs. Concentrate, when learning the stroke, on getting the top edge of your bat to lead the way to the follow-through behind the ear, making sure the wrist does not roll it over.

Hesitation in the swing, a hitch. This habit usually arises from poor timing and/or poor footwork. Part way through his back-swing the player finds himself faced with the realization that the tempo he has selected simply will not do for this particular shot. He finds that he must either speed up the swing or, worse, slow it down so that the bat will arrive at the contact point at the same time as the ball. The result is that his stroke becomes two strokes, one up to the point of realization of his mistake, the other after he adjusts. Some players, rather than setting about correcting their timing, develop a stroke like this and suffer with it as long as they play the game.

The best correction I know requires a firm mental attitude that allows one to practice with the resolve to concentrate only on the follow-through without regard for what happens to the ball after it is hit. By concentrating only on the follow-through, the player is forced to make the stroke as one complete swing, uninterrupted. De-emphasize the actual hitting of the ball and make the stroke flow smoothly from backswing to follow-through. Try to visualize the contact point as far in advance as possible.

Poor footwork. Sometimes in private lessons, when I have a pupil who just can't seem to co-ordinate his footwork so that his left foot steps into the ball at the right moment, I place a ball on the floor three feet behind the table and ask the student to imagine the

Figure 14

Incorrect attacking stroke:
bat turned over after contact

contact point as being waist high above that point. Then I will have him practice approaching that point from different positions on the court. The stationary ball seems to help, for the moving ball is a frightening thing.

Hooking the ball. This is another common bad habit. The player swings at the ball by taking his racket in a path from outside the ball toward the inside, thus putting sidespin on the ball as well as topspin. Except on the serve, and even then only occasionally, sidespin should never be used. Only topspin or underspin is effective in table tennis. On the forehand attack the racket must be brought toward the ball so that at the moment of contact the face of the blade is square to the intended line of flight.

The best corrective for hooking the ball is practice with the penholder grip. This grip almost prohibits swinging from the outside in because of the extreme awkwardness involved in getting the racket head up before contact is made. Regardless of how well your stroke is grooved, a great deal can be gained from practice with the penholder grip. I still practice that way from time to time and afterwards try to adapt my own forehand so that I include in it the best principles of the penholder attack. To cure hooking, for instance, I recommend hitting penholder forehands from the backhand court cross-court to your opponent's backhand. If in practicing this way you remember to keep your elbow close to your body it should result in a swing that is from inside the line of flight toward the outside.

Trying to hit the ball too hard. Even though I stressed the idea of power in the attack I want to make it clear that not every shot can be killed. Knowing your capabilities is very important for winning matches and you must learn to walk before you run. You should endeavor, when learning the forehand drive, to topspin 50 or 100 balls over the net successively at a slow tempo, remembering that a miss at a slow tempo is much worse than a miss when trying for a kill. Missing the table by an inch at a slow tempo is equivalent to missing the table by five feet on a kill shot. In this connection— that is, in trying to achieve steadiness—remember that you must aim. Aim the ball over the net and select a spot on the table that you want to hit to. But here a word of caution: In table tennis the depth of an attacking shot—how close it comes to the table edges— does not make it substantially more difficult to return. On the attack almost the only thing that wins points is speed and most often the attacker must build up his attack during a point so that his opponent will give him a loose ball just a bit higher than it should be on which he will attempt the kill. Therefore, do not practice hitting to the corners. Figure 15 shows the shaded safety zone that your attacking shots should be aimed to. Any ball aimed outside this area will have too little margin for error in return for the insignificant advantage it brings.

This, for the moment, ends the section on the forehand attack. I shall have a few more remarks to make later on the forehand counter-drive, the "loop," and the backhand attack, but for the moment I suggest we turn our attention to defensive play.

Figure 15

The safety zone for attacking shots

CHAPTER 5

Defensive Play

There is no greater satisfaction in the sport than to anticipate an opponent's smash, pump your legs, and from fifteen feet behind the table return a drive that left your opponent's bat at 120 m.p.h. and have it skim back across the net loaded with underspin which forces an error. In a sense the defensive player's art is greater than the attacker's. Being farther away from the table, his target is smaller, and to absorb the shock of hard-hit drives his touch must be as delicate as a violinist's. Moreover, the defensive player has more court to cover than the attacker, for as one retreats away from the table the possible angle that the ball may take increases too, so that at twelve feet behind the table, the defensive player's court may be fifteen feet laterally, whereas the attacker, up close to the table, has only the width of the table, five feet, to worry about.

It should be understood at the outset that defensive play is in itself a method of winning, a style of play. Vienna-born Richard Bergmann had an attack that would have made an average club player ashamed, yet his defense was so impregnable that he became four-times world singles champion. The Oriental ascendancy in the modern game of fast sponge rackets has decreased the interest in learning the defensive game. All over the world, young players try to hit harder and faster than their opponents, without ever thinking of the art of defense. On the other hand, the world-champion Chinese have recently introduced strictly defensive players into their teams and these players have so befuddled and paralyzed the world's best attackers that perhaps a new look in the game will be along shortly. I am not suggesting that the best style of play is defense. I am merely saying that defensive play does not represent cowardice. One should not think of it as an occasional necessity between attacking chances. The player of the future, I feel, will be an all-around player, as comfortable on attack as on defense and thus able to change his style against various opponents.

Forehand Chop Strokes

The defensive shots, called chop strokes, are really extensions of the half-volley shots already described, except that the backswing is longer and more spin is put on the ball. While the half volley is used in answer to a slow return, the chop shots are used in answer to drives or topspin shots. The chop strokes I shall here describe are the ones that I would use in a range of from 4 to 6 feet behind the table.

Let us assume that your opponent begins a point by giving you a fast topspin service (or a topspin drive in answer to one of your half volleys) and that the ball's speed and topspin will carry it so that the ideal interception point will be four feet behind the table. Your opponent has hit his shot from his forehand to yours, the cross-court angle. You are in the ready position and his shot has not surprised you. What to do?

First of all, you cannot return this shot with either a block shot or a half volley. The forehand block is too awkward to make and moreover is not potent enough to present your opponent with any difficulty; the half volley will not do because, as we assumed, the interception point will be four feet behind the table and the half volley, or push, is a close-to-the-table stroke in answer to a push shot. The only alternative is to make either a forehand attacking topspin stroke or a chop shot which says to your opponent in effect, "Go ahead, do something to me." The object of your defensive return is to send the ball back with a chopping motion of the bat through the bottom surface of the ball, which will cause the ball to rotate toward you as it travels toward your opponent. This underspin is necessary for defensive returns since it helps keep the light ball suspended, as it were, and traveling in a straight line. If you have seen a golf ball hit from the tee with a slight backspin that causes it to hug the ground for seventy-five yards and then begin to rise as the spin affects it you will have some notion of how it is possible, from fifteen feet behind a table-tennis table, to slice underneath the ball and have it travel in a straight line, skimming the net by a few inches, and finally settle onto your opponent's court. It is a fine feeling.

As well as keeping the ball afloat during its long flight, underspin makes it harder for your opponent to drive the ensuing shot. Recall for a moment what happened when you practiced the pushing shots against the wall. The slight underspin you applied forced the ball to leave the wall at a much sharper downward angle than it otherwise would have had. Similarly, when the downward pull of your underspin meets your opponent's bat it forces him to play his shot somewhat safer. On the other hand, I must stress here that you should not learn to chop with the intention of developing point-winning strokes through spin. You will of course win points with your spin, particularly when your opponent hits the ball into the net, but do not try to chop the cover off the ball when learning the strokes. Defensive play calls for steadiness. Nevertheless, it does not have to be entirely passive, since you can apply extra spin when you are in perfect control of the particular shot and you can maneuver the attacker into errors too. But essentially, at least when learning, think of defense as passive.

And now for the strokes. We have assumed that the point is beginning with a topspin service from your opponent's forehand to yours. You are in the normal ready position for the return of service—about 2½ to 3 feet behind the table. The ball is coming toward you in a rather high trajectory (for the purposes of learning this shot the serves are being "fed" to you).

Your first job as the ball is hit and approaches you is to properly judge its speed and direction and to "feel" where the ideal contact point will be. This entire matter of timing the shot is a reflex learned through practice. There is no set of rules one can offer as a guide. In general, however, bear in mind that the contact point on defensive shots is lower—farther down on the descending arc—than for attacking shots. The ball must be struck well below the top of the bounce to give its speed a chance to diminish. But remember also that no two shots are hit exactly the same. Each shot calls for an individual adjustment which depends on the speed and, most important, on the trajectory—that is, whether the ball is approaching on a high or a low bounce.

Figure 16a shows the ready position.

Figure 16b shows the initiation of the backswing for the forehand chop. With the elbow tucked firmly in place close to your body, forward of the hip, the first thing that happens on the backswing is that the wrist begins to draw the top edge of the bat up and back into a more cocked position. The cocking of the wrist must be gradual and take place throughout the backswing, so don't snap it into place just as you start your backswing. Draw it back evenly and slowly. As this small amount of wrist action begins, it additionally rolls the racket toward the right so that the face of the blade becomes more open than it was at the ready position. Also, at the first stage of the backswing, there is a shifting of the weight to the left in a smooth pivot which frees the right foot for its step backward and to the right.

Figure 16c shows the backswing midway. The wrist continues its turning to coil the head of the bat, and the forearm, swiveling in the elbow socket, also goes back. But note that the hinge, the elbow, stays forward of the hip. It does *not* move back as the forearm moves back. It is a fixed hinge upon which the forearm swings.

Since we have decided that this serve you are returning has a high trajectory, the path that your racket takes as you draw it back must be upward toward your right shoulder. And it will follow the identical path downward as you approach the ball on the forward swing. For balls that approach on a lower trajectory the path of the backswing will be more parallel to the floor.

Notice too in Figure 16c that the right foot is shifting back. This retreat is almost perfectly synchronized with the backswing so that the racket blade and the right foot go back in unison and the right foot is planted in position at the same time the racket reaches the top of the backswing. Note the bending of the body, the cock of the head to the right, and the height and extension of the left hand.

Figure 16d shows the backswing complete. The top edge of the bat has led the way back and, aside from the initial opening of the racket face, there has been no additional "rolling over." The wrist has been cocked so that the handle of the bat points toward the table at a downward angle. This is a minimum amount of wrist cock. If I were in perfect position for a shot I might coil the wrist still more, so that the handle pointed off toward the right; for the amount of spin one can apply is determined by how much the wrist is cocked on the backswing. If the wrist is cocked so little that the handle points toward the left at the top of the backswing, only

Figure 16

The forehand chop

the forearm is left to accelerate the bat, doing the work the wrist should have done, with a consequent loss of fine control and "bite" at the moment of impact.

Figure 16e shows the start of the forward swing. This takes place without any pause at the top of the backswing and is initiated merely by an unpivoting from the hips. The right arm and wrist are still maintained in the full backswing position even though they have been dragged forward a bit by this preliminary uncoiling toward the left. By delaying the arm and wrist action we allow additional acceleration into the ball later on by having them catch up.

Figure 16f shows that the wrist and the forearm have now joined the action. With the elbow still forward of the hips and acting as a stationary hinge, the forearm swings forward on it. At the same time, the wrist begins to uncoil, moving the head of the bat into the ball. It is important to note that the blade is now descending along the exact same alley it moved in during the backswing. Again there is no wavering or scooping. The plane of the blade remains fixed in whatever angle was determined by the backswing.

Figure 16g shows the contact point. If you have timed the shot correctly the wrist will, just at the moment of impact, firmly move the head of the bat into the ball, descending downward through the back surface with a biting action that seems to keep going until it is abruptly halted at the end of the follow-through. This movement of the wrist at the moment of impact is, of course, the crucial moment in the swing. It is the downward blow of the head of the bat that imparts the spin, and it must be precisely measured. If the ball is not sliced finely enough, the forward motion of the stroke will carry the ball beyond the table on your opponent's side. On the other hand, too fine a cut will give you a great deal of spin, but the ball may merely rise straight up without reaching the net or, worse, you may miss the ball entirely.

Notice that at the contact point the wrist has taken the head of the bat forward so that the handle of the bat is parallel to the rear table edge. Also note that the ball has been struck at a point even with the left foot, the forward foot. This is an absolute rule for defensive play: never allow the ball to get behind you.

Figure 16h shows the position midway through the follow-through. The wrist continues to uncoil, maintaining the tension, and the forearm, still swiveling on the hinge of the elbow, straightens out relative to the upper arm. The pivot is taking the weight toward the left side and there is the feeling that the right heel is being raised from the floor. The head remains cocked sideways as the ball is still sighted with the left eye.

A word about the position of the ball. Though the stroke has almost been completed, the ball is still close to the contact point. In other words, the racket head, slicing through the ball, moves forward faster than the ball itself. At the termination of the follow-through the ball will still not have cleared the net.

Figure 16i shows the completion of the shot. The head of the bat reaches its final position with an abrupt halt, almost as though it had met something solid. Once the head of the bat finds its resting place there is no further movement toward the left by the arm or body. Notice that the wrist has not been held back; the head of the bat, the handle, the forearm, and the upper arm all point toward the center of the table. At the end of a well-timed shot you should have the feeling that you have wedged your bat into a sturdy tree. What this really means is that the tension you developed at the moment of impact stayed with the shot all the way. A relaxed, flabby follow-through is a sign that the ball has not been struck with real "bite."

Though I have tried to analyze the action of the forehand chop stroke rather carefully by breaking it down into its component motions, the swing is not really complicated—especially if you have already mastered to some extent the forehand half volley I described earlier. The main difference between the half volley and the chop is the feeling of the extra tension and the more vigorous swing. The half volley, which answers a similar return by your opponent, must be limited in its briskness. Because a half volley by your opponent carries little forward motion, too severe a wrist action as you strike the ball will send it into the bleachers. On the other hand, even a moderately paced topspin service, such as we have here tackled, will approach with enough forward motion so that a crisp slice through the bottom surface will send it back relatively slowly.

The Backhand Defense

As I have pointed out, at even the highest levels of play the backhand attack is not so potent a weapon as the forehand attack. Indeed, the game's best attacking players, the Orientals, shun the backhand offense so much that they run countless extra yards during a match covering, with their potent forehand attack, shots that are hit to their backhand side. Not every player can be as fleet-footed as the Orientals, however, and so the lack of backhand attack (which seems inherent in the game) means that the backhand defense is, possibly, more crucial than the forehand defense.

Following the system I used for the forehand chop, let's analyze the stroke for the backhand chop.

We will assume that your opponent is serving and begins the point with a moderately high bounding service toward your left with sufficient pace in it to make its ideal contact point about four feet behind the table.

You are in the ready position, of course, for the return of service:
the left hand is up; the right wrist is cocked slightly holding the
racket head up; the legs are slightly bent at the knees and the body
weight is forward. You are alert and expectant.

The service has been hit to your left side but not so wide as to
require two steps to reach it. For the purpose of concentrating on
the stroke, let's assume you can reach it comfortably with only one
step of the left foot.

Figure 17a shows the first phase of the backswing. Actually,
nothing has changed here except that the body has begun its
pivot to the left. Just after this preliminary movement the left foot
will make its step and the forearm will be drawn back. But here
only the hips and shoulders have turned.

Figure 17b shows the step toward the left rear and the drawing
back of the forearm. Pay particular attention to the way the forearm
is brought back. Notice that the right elbow is held high and
pointed toward the net. This is crucial. The high, extended elbow
provides the hinge upon which the forearm will swing. Figure 17b
shows additionally that the wrist is now coiling up to cock the
racket head. The body is inclined to the left.

Figure 17c shows the completion of the backswing. The racket
has been drawn back (not swung back) with a feeling of tension
in the forearm and wrist. The top edge of the racket has been
drawn back first, and there has been no wavering or scooping or
changing of the plane of the face of the blade once the racket takes
its backward path. The wrist coils up and you have the feeling
that if the racket and your arm were extended, they would be coiled
right around your body. Here, however, the racket has been drawn
back in an upward path and it stops almost touching the left
shoulder. (To return shots with a lower trajectory the racket would
be drawn back more parallel to the floor and the body would be in
more of a crouch.)

Figure 17d shows the initiation of the forward swing. This is made
without pausing at the top of the backswing and is begun by
turning the hips toward the right. Then, almost simultaneously,
the wrist begins turning the head of the bat into the ball as the
forearm begins to swing downward. The downward path here is
approximately 45 degrees and it follows exactly the path that was
taken for the backswing. Pay particular attention to the curve in

the wrist away from the forearm. This provides the tension in the swing and must be maintained throughout the stroke, including, as you shall see, the follow-through.

Figure 17*e* shows the position just before impact. The wrist has now turned the head of the bat downward so that at impact a line drawn between the racket head and the handle would be horizontal. If you consider the stroke as a semicircle, the contact should be made midway for maximum power. (Maximum power is desirable even though the ball will not be hit hard. The racket face will graze through the bottom surface of the ball.)

Notice too in Figure 17*e* that the blade is held by the cocked wrist at an angle that inclines it toward the outside hemisphere of the ball. That is, if you think of the ball as divided vertically into two halves, the blade strikes the left half first, then completes its semicircle toward the right.

Figure 17*f* shows the contact, made with a firm punch into the ball with the head of the bat. But the ball, of course, must be grazed only, as if in an attempt to remove its bottom skin. The ability to slice thin will come through practice, not through changing the stroke.

Notice that the contact has been made forward of the body above the right foot. The feeling is that the ball has fallen into the pocket you have prepared for it and that pocket is in front of you, not behind you. If hard-hit drives are allowed to climb up over your shoulder, so to speak, you will not be able to generate enough power with the backswing to compensate for the forward speed of the ball. The ball must be trapped before it has a chance to get behind the body.

In Figure 17*g*, the wrist and forearm continue to uncoil evenly. The bottom edge of the bat leads the way, threading the same alley that the bat took on its backswing. There is no scooping or changing of the plane of the racket face. As the bat moves forward the body completes its pivot in place. This is merely a turning of the hips and shoulders to the right. There is no leaning into the ball.

Figure 17*h* shows the completed follow-through. Notice that the wrist still maintains its curve relative to the forearm. The head of the bat has been turning throughout the swing on its wrist hinge and is now pointed in the same direction as the forearm—that is, toward the net. This is a particularly important checkpoint. If you

Figure 17

The backhand chop

have held back on the turning of the wrist, say for reasons of imagined safety, the head of the bat will still be, at the completion of the follow-through, pointed toward the left. This is dead wrong. Better to miss the shot completely than develop this bad habit. For power, spin, and "touch," the head of the bat must be used at the moment of impact. So check your follow-through to see that the upper arm, forearm, wrist, and racket head are all lined up.

At the completion of the follow-through there is no longer any bend at the elbow. Again you should have the feeling that the

stroke has ended abruptly, as though you have wedged your bat into a block of wood.

The illustrations above, as I explained, cover the forehand and backhand chops in answer to medium-speed topspin attacks where the ideal contact point is 4 to 6 feet behind the table; the kind of defense used in answering a service, for instance. But as your ability and the strength of your opponents become greater you will meet situations that will force you to retreat even farther away from the table to defend hard-hit balls. Essentially, your chopping strokes will be the same as for medium-speed attacks, but they will have to be adapted somewhat. Here are the few basic rules to remember:

To return hard-hit shots, the first requirement is to give yourself plenty of room behind the table. You cannot handle a hard-hit shot when standing four feet behind the table because your reflexes are not fast enough to make a controlled shot with so little time. You must allow the ball to slow down by intercepting it later. When I am in defensive position against a consistent attacker I usually allow about ten feet between me and the table edge. Other players allow twelve or thirteen feet. This does not mean that I stand that far back to return service, of course. It means that if I am on the defensive end of a particular point I try to give the ball about 19 feet in which to slow down. It is far easier to run forward, toward the table, to return a particular shot that comes somewhat slower in a rally than to dart back to return an unexpectedly hard shot. Thus, if I have decided to play a particular point defensively, I do not try to get back to the table after having retreated. Rather, I maintain my ten-foot position until my opponent forces me in closer with an easier drive or perhaps a drop shot.

Taking the ball farther behind the table means taking it lower, usually, than the chops we illustrated for use in the 4- to 6-foot range. Therefore, instead of taking the racket back and swinging down in a 45-degree angle as we did for the closer shots, the racket must be swung more parallel to the floor. Since the ball is intercepted lower, what you are trying to do, essentially, is to get farther underneath the ball by opening the face of the racket more.

Figure 18 illustrates the backswing, contact point, and follow-through positions for the deep defensive forehand chop. Figure 19 illustrates the same positions for the backhand chop. Notice that in

Figure 18

The deep defensive forehand chop

these shots the body is crouched more in an effort to get down to the ball.

In your first attempts to return hard-hit low, bouncing balls from ten feet behind the table you will no doubt find that when you open the blade of your bat to get more underneath the ball, the ball will rebound higher than you anticipated. This can be corrected only through practice. If I am in perfect position for a shot I can skim the ball over the net by chopping through it with a perfectly flat blade. My feeling then is that I am making the same motion that I would make if I were trying to pitch a flat stone over water. But the opening of my racket varies with each shot, and the feeling of the correct angle must be learned through experience.

In private coaching I find that the most common errors in making the defensive strokes are:

Improper timing. There is no cure-all for poor timing. The only thing I can do is again stress that on defensive shots the ball must be taken lower than on attacking shots. The ball must be contacted as it descends and the contact point must be in front of your body. Try to imagine when practicing that you are carrying near your body a pocket, or hoop, or basket that the ball must fall into. Adjust your timing so that your stroke contacts the ball just as it falls into the pocket. The pocket is always on a line with your forward foot, remember, and thus, by striking the ball always at the same distance in front of your body, your timing will get grooved. If your legs do not take you into position you will be handling one shot too far in front of you and the next one behind you, so that no strict timing can be enforced and you will be constantly improvising.

There are, incidentally, some players who prefer to take the ball behind the body when playing defense and usually their strokes resemble a floor-sweeping motion. This type of defense can often produce fine retrieving players, but the main trouble with allowing the ball to get behind you is that you sacrifice the chance of getting heavy spin. In the modern sponge attacking game, if the defensive player can win at all, he cannot win merely by retrieving in the hope of outsteadying his opponent. He must be able, instead, to contain the attacker with heavy spin and *force* him to miss.

Failure to make a complete stroke. Beginners all too often try to do too much at one time during practice. If you practice with the intention of being very consistent your perfection of the stroke will almost certainly be delayed. At the beginning, practice the

Figure 19

The deep defensive backhand chop

stroke only and ignore the number of errors you make. If, instead, you practice with the intent of becoming ultra-steady you will no doubt end by developing a stroke that to you seems safer but actually is not. For instance, beginners imagine that by holding back the wrist on the defensive shots, or by pushing the forearm into the ball rather than by swinging it in, they can get additional control. For beginners, this may actually be true, since they are playing for the most part against players of their own caliber. But as the strength of your opponents increases you will find that holding back on the strokes makes your returns weaker and, against the increased speed of your opponent's drives, actually unsteadier as well.

Figure 20a shows the position of a follow-through when the wrist has been held back.

Figure 20b represents the correct follow-through position: note the full follow-through of the wrist.

Drawing the elbow away from the body (particularly behind the back). Once again I must stress that the elbow is the hinge upon which the forearm swings and throughout the stroke (either backhand or forehand) it must be kept forward of the body. If the elbow is allowed to roam behind the body on the forehand chop, the forearm can only swing sideways from left to right, not forward into the ball. On the backhand, of course, the elbow cannot be taken behind the body, but it is equally wrong to let the elbow (on the backhand chop) get too close to the body. On the backhand, keep the elbow suspended and pointed toward the shot.

Hitting across the ball from the outside in. Before I show you the cure for this I must make sure you understand the error.

Ideally, the stroke, from the top of the backswing to the end of the follow-through, should describe a semicircle. For maximum power, as I have explained, contact should be made midway. On the first half of the semicircle the bat should go outward toward the ball, striking it, as it were, from the inside out. If, on the other hand, the bat is held wide of the body on the backswing and not kept close to the shoulder, the result is that the bat will strike the ball incorrectly by moving across it from the outside in.

In other words, on the backhand side you will be dragging your racket across the ball from left to right; and on the forehand side you will be dragging the racket from right to left. In both cases you will get sidespin on the ball as well as underspin. And, as I have stated in the introductory chapter, sidespin is never

Figure 20

The (a) incorrect and (b) correct wrist positions on
the follow-through of the forehand defensive stroke

employed by the experts. We want either direct forward spin for the drives or direct underspin for the chops. (Figure 21 shows correct and incorrect racket angles for forehand and backhand defense.)

This error of dragging across the ball from the outside in is usually the result of not releasing the head of the bat into the ball and it can usually be overcome by deliberately concentrating on moving the wrist just before the moment of impact. Another good way of correcting the fault is to compensate for it by trying deliberately to hit outside the ball. Thus, if you imagine the approaching ball divided into two hemispheres by a vertical seam, try to make your stroke so that the head of your bat strikes the hemisphere farthest away from your body: the right half on the forehand, and the left half on the backhand. But be sure, in so doing, that your racket head *first passes* the inner hemisphere.

For example, when I am playing well, I often deliberately chop on the outside of the ball for extra bite (this does not give sidespin) and have the feeling when making the stroke that I am *curling* the head of the bat around the outside half of the ball. In Figure 21, *a* and *b* (forehand and backhand respectively) show the angle of the bat at contact when the ball is hit correctly, slightly on the outside; *c* and *d* show the incorrect, outside-in contact angle.

Some General Notes on Defensive Play

Once you have learned the basic motions of the forehand and backhand push shots that I described in the first chapters you are on the way toward developing your defensive game, for the chop shots, as I have shown, are merely extensions of the pushing shots. The difference is one of quality, not of character. But one must progress slowly and achieve a good deal of ball control with the pushing shots before going on to the chop shots. One of the reasons for my success in the game, I have always felt, is that for the first two years I played the game I played a basement style, standing up close to the table and pushing the ball back without any spin at all. To me, the object of the game was "not to miss" and it never occurred to me that there could be such things as chops and drives. Thus, when I discovered my first table-tennis club at thirteen, and saw the game played as a sport, I already had such good ball control that my strokes developed quite rapidly.

For the average player who cannot spend two years pushing

Figure 21

The (a) correct and (c) incorrect racket angles
for forehand defense; the (b) correct and
(d) incorrect racket angles for backhand defense

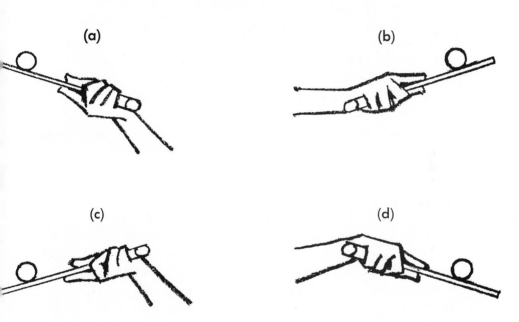

(a) (b)

(c) (d)

balls over the net I recommend the following steps for learning
defensive play.

Out of every playing session, try to set aside some time for practice. Match play may be more fun, but the will to win often prevents the development of the strokes. The exercise against the wall
that you use for the push shots may also be used for the chop shots,
with the corresponding extra speed of the ball and the extra
distance away from the table. Vary this wall exercise with practice
against the medium-speed topspin service described in this chapter;
for this is the intermediate stage of your defense, between the push
and the return of hard-hit drives. Your buddy, ideally, should feed
you many serves at one tempo until you have mastered that particular pace. Then, somewhat faster, lower serves should be tried, bear-
ing in mind, as the tempo increases, that your object is to get the
ball over the net by using the proper stroke. You must constantly
check your backswing and follow-through positions to guard

against self-deception—holding the wrist back, for instance, to play the ball safe. This practice method can be varied so that the services are fed alternately to the backhand and then to the forehand sides, but, at the beginning, two or three dozen serves to the same place at the same tempo is the best method to pursue.

Do not try to chop the cover off the ball. As I have stressed, the defensive game is one of consistency. A miss of an easy serve is a far greater error than a miss when trying for a risky but potential point-winning kill. Only when you are absolutely certain that you have complete control over the particular shot you are executing should you attempt to make your chop more active—and by more active I mean, of course, adding spin. So, to insure the early cultivation of this habit, I recommend that when practicing your chopping strokes, you return the ball in the same rhythm established by your buddy's practice serve. If he gives you a slow, high-moving service, make your return follow the same trajectory and with the same tempo. When he increases his tempo, increase yours to the same extent. Remember, you must get your wrist and racket head through the ball even though you may be only hitting the ball softly. When you increase the tempo of the shot, it is the racket head that gets most of the additional acceleration and thus adds the spin.

Without expecting you to become a ballet dancer it is still necessary to state again that without proper footwork the right defensive strokes cannot be made. If you have to reach for every shot, or hurry your backswing, you will never have control. The importance of footwork becomes clear if you think of your stroke as merely a grooved mechanical device that automatically puts the ball on the table when the lever (the racket head) strikes it. But to keep the lever in its groove for balls that are landing on all parts of the table, your legs, like wheels, must roll the lever to the proper position.

However many steps you may take to get into position for a particular chop, backhand or forehand, remember that almost always the final step before impact, the step that is synchronized with the backswing, will be a backward leaning step to the side with the rear foot. On the forehand chop that step will be with the right foot; and on the backhand that step will be with the left foot. The step should almost never be forward toward the ball, but on those occasions when you are too far behind the contact point, and you *must* come forward to recover the ball, the final step should be with the left foot for the forehand, and the right foot for the backhand, as only in this way can you achieve a sideways position during the stroke.

During the ready position, keep your weight forward (though not so much that it is being supported only by the balls of the feet) and develop the sense of alertness so necessary to defensive play. Also, make your steps around the court short, fast ones rather than long, lazy ones. Long steps do not allow you to achieve the precise position that short ones do. Furthermore, long steps are usually accompanied by long, lazy movements of the arm, which, as we have seen, is far from desirable. Even a few little hops up and down, *in place,* will help you get ready to move on the defense. Quick-stepping footwork and firm decisive strokes are the ideal.

Another point I wish to re-emphasize in connection with footwork is the feeling that the ball is going to drop into a "pocket" you have prepared for it. Trying to establish that pocket at the same place relative to your legs and body for every shot is merely another way of saying "get into position."

Beginners often develop faulty defensive strokes because of the misapprehension that when they chop downward at the ball, the ball rolls upward along the rubber facing of the bat before it rebounds. Consequently, I've seen many players who deliberately tried to hit the ball so that it struck the bat below center, thinking that it would roll up toward the center because the bat was moving downward. This is dead wrong. With a firm, brisk stroke the ball leaves the bat immediately and no attempt should be made to compensate for any imagined roll. Furthermore, the notion that this rolling action, if it could be attained, would increase the spin is also incorrect. The amount of spin is determined by the fineness of the slice and by the speed with which the racket head grazes the ball.

Finally, I wish to set straight another common mistaken notion. The defensive player should not try to vary his returns as far as depth is concerned. That is, he should not try to place them closer to the net or closer to the rear edge of the table from one shot to the next. Chop shots (and drives for that matter, too), though they may be hit in various directions from right to left on the table, should never be varied as to depth. In terms of depth, they should be hit as close as possible to the center of the *safest* area. And that safest area seems to be from 12 to 18 inches in front of the rear edge of the table. Thus, a ball falling into the safest depth on the table would land 15 inches from the rear edge and 39 inches from the net. (The table is 9 feet long and 5 feet in width.)

This feeling of depth will become automatic after a while and will give you the maximum chance for steadiness. True, some shots will fall beyond, or in front of, this safest area, but by trying for that area on every shot, only extreme miscalculation will take the ball into the net or off the table.

Incidentally, chop shots that land close to the net are easier for the attacker to put away than those falling in the safe area. Figure 15 shows the target area for defensive players. Note that this is the same target area as for attacking players.

In the section dealing with tactics I shall have a few more comments concerning the defense, but for the present I trust I have given the aspiring player enough to work on.

CHAPTER 6

The Service

I have deliberately delayed discussing the most elementary shot in the game, the service. For the intermediate or advanced player, a description of service technique seemed needless. For the beginner, since the service strokes are unique, I felt that too early a description of them might conflict with the development of the more important strokes, particularly the forehand drive.

The newcomer to the sport, particularly the basement player anxious to learn the strokes, is astounded to find out how relatively unimportant the serve is in table tennis. Though I have discussed the fine points of the game with fellow players at tournaments all over the world I cannot ever remember seriously discussing a player's serve. The server's advantage in the modern game is minimal.

Unlike lawn tennis, in which the serve is delivered directly across the net, in table tennis the serve must, before it crosses the net, bounce on the server's side of the table. The amount of power that can be applied, therefore, is quite limited. Moreover, after the ban on fingerspin serves in the 1930's and the ban on racket-rubbing serves in the 1940's, the amount of spin one can apply is also severely limited. Prior to those rule changes the server was allowed to spin the ball in his fingers before striking it, or hold it steady in his fingers to prolong contact as the bat rubbed against the firmly clutched ball. Nowadays, the ball must be held on the palm of the hand, thrown into the air, and then struck. This, of course, prevents the serve from being a point winner in its own right, though the Oriental masters of the game have shown recently that with continuous variation of the type of serve they use in a match they can keep opponents off balance and often pick up a half dozen points per game when their opponents either miss the serve outright or set up the service return. In international play I would guess that an average of five points a game can be attributed to the serve.

The two most important serves to learn are the fast topspin serve made with the forehand, and the chop serve made with either backhand or forehand.

The Forehand Topspin Serve

This is the serve you use when it is your intention to take the initiative, to attack on your opponent's return of service. Let us assume, for example, that you are facing a player who will yield the attack to you if your service can generate enough speed to force him into a defensive reply. Let's assume further that your opponent is primarily a one-wing attacker having a good forehand drive but not much of a backhand drive. Your course, then, is clear. You must deliver as fast a topspin serve as you can make *with absolute safety* and be prepared to control the attack upon your opponent's probable chop return.

For this serve I take the stance shown in Figure 22a. This stance you will recognize immediately as being very close to the stance one would take for the forehand drive, but the similarity between the serve and the drive ends there, for the stroke is actually quite different.

Figure 22a shows the body positioned sideways toward the table, left side forward. The knees are slightly bent. The left foot is pointed directly toward the net and the right foot is angled outward at 45 degrees. The right elbow is held quite close to the hip, and the racket head is held up and back with almost a right angle formed by the back of the hand and the forearm. For the serve the control of the bat is in the hand, just as it is for every stroke in the game. You should be able to shake the racket head up and down with the wrist only, just as though it were a hammer. The ball rests on the palm of the left hand, which also is cocked at the wrist, and held waist high. The bat and the ball are about ten inches apart at this point.

The toss should be made with as smooth a motion as possible. The motion is initiated by an upward movement of the forearm and upper arm moving together as a unit. Following this, the left wrist gently uncocks to toss the ball into the air.

At the same time the right hand has taken the bat back to the position shown in Figure 22*b*. Very little has changed from the ready position. But note that the forearm has swiveled back in the elbow socket (the elbow is still held against the hip) and the wrist has been cocked a bit further back.

The toss should project the ball about six inches upward. It may also take the ball slightly toward the rear—that is, toward the right shoulder. Too low a toss will force you to hurry the swing; too high a toss will increase the speed of the falling ball and make it harder to time.

Figure 22*c* shows the ball descending. The right forearm, swinging in the elbow socket, moves forward. The attempt is to strike the ball as it descends, perhaps two inches off the top of the throw. All this time, notice, the face of the bat is square to the net, at right angles to the floor.

You will see here that unlike the wrist action for the forehand drive where the racket head must be pointed *downward* prior to contact, the forehand topspin service is made with the wrist moving the racket head parallel to the table surface. The difference is that the forehand drive is essentially an underhand swing designed to get maximum topspin on the ball to force it down as it crosses the net, while the serve is made with more of a sidearm swing in which the topspin is applied by rolling the racket head over the back top surface of the ball. This is made with a wrist tap, and it is as close to a slap as you will find in table tennis.

Figure 22*d* shows the contact. The wrist is turning the racket head up and over the ball. The momentum will take the bat across the body from right to left to the follow-through position.

Figure 22*e* shows the follow-through position for the forehand topspin serve. Contrast this with the forehand drive follow-through in which the bat must finish on the *right* side of the body, behind the ear.

This fast forehand service can be made to the forehand court as well. To do this, merely shift the entire ready position to the left and follow the stroke described above.

The topspin serve should strike the table farther out toward the rear edge than either the chop or the drive. But do not try for too much extra length because the service, since it probably will not

Figure 22

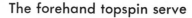

The forehand topspin serve

win any points for you outright against a competent opponent, must be played as an absolutely safe shot. The service should *never* be hit into the net or off the table—and I mean *never*. Tournament players rarely serve a fault from one season to the next.

In the modern sponge game, the extreme grippiness of the bat makes it possible to reverse any spin that one's opponent puts on the ball and still maintain control. Contrastingly, in the days when all players used normal pimpled rubber, it was very risky to chop a chop or topspin a topspin, which meant reversing the spin. Almost always, a chop was topspinned, and a topspin was chopped, which was merely *continuing* the spin. But the sponge bat changed all that and consequently the aggressive fast topspin serve, to which a defensive chop was almost always the response, can nowadays

boomerang when the receiver takes the attack with a counter-topspin.

It is therefore practical against many attacking players to rely on an underspin serve. The virtue of the underspin serve is that it is made with a chop stroke and can thus be kept closer to the net than can the topspin serve, since the slicing blow of the chop imparts less forward motion to the ball than does the more direct contact of the topspin.

Keeping the ball close to the net gives the server a distinct advantage against certain types of players. When playing against the speedy, counter-driving Orientals, for example, I invariably use a chop serve rather than a topspin. By keeping the chop serve close to the net I am almost certain to receive a defensive reply in the form of a half volley. True, the receiver can also keep the ball close

Figure 23

The forehand chop serve

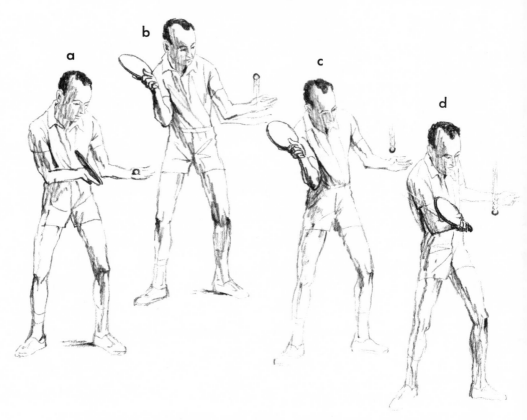

to the net on his return, but it is more difficult for him to do this than for the server.

Figure 23*a* shows the ready position for the forehand-chop serve to the center of the table. This is the same position as the ready position for the topspin serve, except that here the blade of the bat is tilted back so that the face is quite open. During the stroke this open face will chop downward, slicing the ball well below its center. Another slight difference in the ready position is that the left and right hands are closer together.

In Figure 23*b* as the ball reaches the height of the six-inch toss, the forearm, from the elbow, is taken up and back at a 45-degree angle. There is also an additional cocking of the wrist. Notice that at the top of the backswing for this forehand-chop serve the elbow is still hugging the waist, while the upper arm, from shoulder to elbow, remains almost vertical and hanging without tension. Whatever tension there is (there is relatively little) is felt in the hand and wrist.

Figure 23c shows the initiation of the downward swing which began just as the ball fell from the top of the toss. There is a slight pivot, turning the right shoulder toward the ball, and the wrist begins to uncoil. The elbow stays close to the body.

Figure 23d shows the position just before impact. The wrist, which was cocked, now moves forward smoothly so that the head of the bat can catch up with the swing and meet the ball squarely.

Figure 23e shows the moment of impact and Figure 23f shows the position just after impact. Here you see that the forearm begins to straighten out. Up to this point the forearm and upper arm formed a V, but the momentum of the stroke straightens the arm out until the forearm and upper arm form a straight line as in Figure 23g and the wrist ends the action with a brisk snap into its follow-through position.

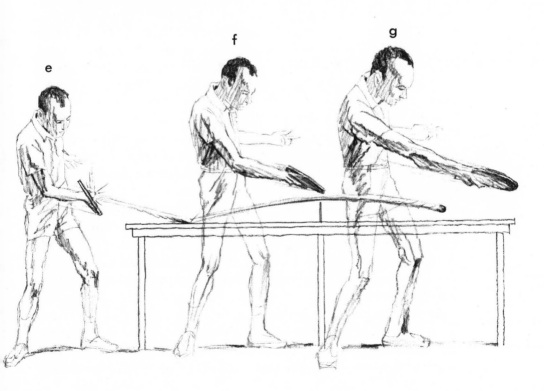

I must re-emphasize my statement that service is relatively unimportant in table tennis. By and large, the fancier the service the poorer the player, which is only another way of saying that inexperienced players try to develop potent serves in the mistaken notion that they can be automatic point winners. At best, a severely spun serve makes the receiver a bit more cautious, but seldom can it force an error. Indeed, were I to miss the serve of the world champion, I would feel ashamed of myself.

Nonetheless, I am going to include here two more service variations which can be very effective against inexperienced players. For those of you who play the basement game I can promise you that a little practice of the following serves will pull many matches out for you.

The first is a serve made with a combination of topspin and sidespin. The serve is illustrated in Figure 24. Note particularly the ready position, which is a crouch. This enables the server to contact the ball closer to the table surface and keep the ball on a low trajectory. More wrist is used in this serve than for any other. During the stroke the wrist twists the racket head from left to right over the top outside surface of the ball with a brisk snap of the wrist just at the moment of impact. This is similar to an American twist serve in lawn tennis. Inexperienced opponents will almost always hit this service off the table to their left because of the sidespin.

Another good sidespin serve is illustrated in Figure 25. Note that the racket is drawn behind the ball from right to left, the racket moves parallel to the floor, and pure sidespin is put on the ball without chop or topspin being added. This serve will force an opponent to hit toward his right unless he compensates for the spin.

Note: Though sidespin is occasionally effective in serving, it should *never* be used in any other stroke in the game (except the trace of outside spin I spoke of when making the chop). At all times, for chopping and driving, you should strive for pure underspin or pure topspin. The use of sidespin takes away from these vital spins that give control, since to achieve sidespin the head of the racket must move across the ball, thus compromising the forward or reverse spin.

The topspin and chop services can be made with either the backhand or the forehand. For the backhand-chop serve use the stroke one would use for a close-to-the-table chop; for the backhand topspin service, use the stroke illustrated in Figure 26 for the backhand pickup counter-drive.

I recommend, however, that the forehand serves be developed first, since practice on the forehand side will improve and strengthen your most important shot, the forehand drive.

Figure 25

The sidespin serve

CHAPTER 7

Other Strokes

Your repertoire of strokes is now almost complete. There remain only the backhand drive, the forehand counter-drive, and the drop shot. By this time you should have a firm grasp of the principles of timing, pivoting, and the ability to swing fluidly, so it will not be necessary to do a painstaking analysis of these strokes. Let's begin, then, with the backhand pickup counter-drive, which, in the modern game, is the most important backhand attacking stroke.

Pickup Counter-Drive

The pickup counter-drive is used to maintain the attack when your opponent tries to take it away from you by hitting a hard topspin drive to your backhand side.

As I have said previously, the Orientals, with their incredible footwork, can handle with their forehands even fast drives that bounce to their extreme left; and they are so quick that they can get back into position to cover their exposed forehand flank in the event their opponents try to pass them on that side with a counter-drive. Indeed, one of the ways to beat the Oriental game is to crowd them into their backhand corner and, while they are hitting forehands from there, counter-drive down the line to their forehand side. The only trouble with this system is that from their backhand corner the penholders can hit their most effective shot; a forehand cross-court shot that goes to their opponent's backhand. Thus, unless one is armed with a superb defense, a strong counter-drive on the backhand is vital.

Since most of you will not be playing in the World Championships in the near future, the Oriental hegemony need not upset you, but it is worthwhile nonetheless to know how to play against their style since many Western players using the shakehands grip try to imitate them—that is, covering the entire court with the forehand drive.

I want to stress at the beginning that the backhand counter-drive (unlike the forehand counter-drive) should not be thought of as a point-winning stroke. It is an emergency shot that keeps your attack going until you can gain position to hit your more potent forehand drive.

The trouble with the backhand drive in table tennis is that the arm must stretch across the body to the left to reach the ball and is thus deprived of the longer backswing that one can take on the forehand side where one can stretch *behind* the body. This means that to get any real power on the backhand attack a great deal of wrist snap must go into the shot to compensate for the lack of backswing and forearm momentum. And snapping the wrist hard enough to matter leads to a loss of control. Thus, of all the world's great players, I can think of only two who were stronger on the backhand attack than on the forehand: the Hungarians Victor Barna and Ferenc Sido.

Let's assume that you have begun a point with a fast topspin service to your opponent's backhand. But instead of chopping it back, as you expected, he surprises you by quickly topspinning the ball back with his backhand. His shot comes cross-court to your backhand.

Figure 26 illustrates the typical backhand counter-drive made close to the table. Since the counter-drive is made in answer to a fast attacking shot, there is no real ready position. The action takes place so fast that there is no time for your legs to take you to a waiting position. Thus, in Figure 26a, the body is facing the table in a square stance, not the sideways stance that is used for the forehand drive. Also notice that the only backswing necessary is to get the forearm and elbow poised as shown.

Also, in Figure 26a, notice that, unlike the forehand drive, the backhand drive shown here does not start with the head of the racket down and the wrist bent back. On the contrary, the wrist is kept well up with almost the same angle formed between it and the forearm as was needed for the forehand drive.

Figure 26b shows the path of the swing as it approaches the ball. The head of the racket leads the swing on this backhand drive, and

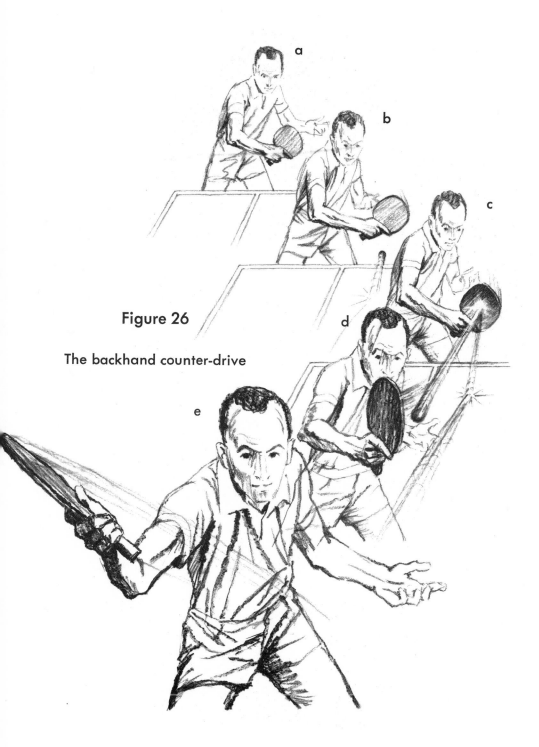

Figure 26

The backhand counter-drive

this is done by initiating the swing with a flicking forward of the wrist. Crucial to the entire shot is getting the racket squarely behind the ball before swinging.

Figure 26c shows the impact. The head of the bat is turning over the top surface of the ball in a brisk, short wrist movement. There should be no feeling of rubbing the ball to get topspin. Since this ball is being taken low, on the pickup *before* it reaches the top of the bounce, it cannot be hit as hard as a kill shot. So don't worry about the topspin. The angle of your bat, which is more or less trapping the ball, and the natural grippiness of the sponge surface will take the ball back easily.

Figure 26d shows the position midway in the short follow-through. Notice that the path of the bat is taking it across the body toward the right side; but this is peculiar to the backhand, remember, and should never be incorporated into the forehand stroke where the bat must finish on the same side of the body, behind the right ear.

Figure 26e shows the follow-through completed. The wrist has taken the racket head over so that the face of the bat is angled toward the floor and the handle points toward the left foot.

The timing of the shot will take some practice since this is one of the few shots in the game where the ball is taken on the rise. The reason for taking the ball on the rise is to gain an advantage in time, not because the shot is better controlled this way. But, because the ball is taken so low relative to the net, only limited power can be used. In one sense you can think of this shot as a kind of elementary block shot with some topspin added.

Once the timing has been solved, this pickup counter-drive in answer to a topspin shot to the backhand is quite easy to execute—particularly with the sponge bat. Almost any stroke that manages to turn the top of the bat over the ball at the right time will accomplish it, for there seems to be something inherent in the sponge bat that makes it a natural counter-driving weapon. The pickup drive, for example, cannot be made successfully against a chopped return. Nine times out of ten, the underspin will force your ball into the net when you try to take the ball on the rise.

Use this shot only when necessary, and then only for maneuvering, not for point-winning. In general, this shot should be hit cross-court to your opponent's backhand. He, likewise, may counter-drive, using the identical pickup stroke, and so a series of quick backhand exchanges may develop until one player or the other commits an error or steps into position quickly enough to hit a forehand drive which, with the other player trapped up to the table, should be a winner.

The backhand counter-drive from *behind* the table may be made by using the same stroke as above. Instead of taking the ball on the pickup, however, a behind-the-table counter-drive—say from four feet behind the table—implies a certain advantage in the time one will have to prepare for the shot. Therefore, when executing the counter-drive from a deeper range, it is possible to take a small circular backswing with the forearm which will give additional power. Since the ball is not going to be trapped on the pickup, but hit away from the table and struck higher on the bounce, it is quite possible to make this shot a point winner. There is no limit to how hard the ball can be hit; the only limit is that of maintaining control.

For counter-driving a backhand from a position behind the table the contact point may be anywhere on the ball's trajectory: the rise, the top of the bounce, or the fall. For maximum power and control, it is my opinion that once again the ball should be taken just off the top of the bounce.

Hitting a backhand drive against chop calls for a different stroke, though not a radically different one. For one thing, the face of the racket, which on the counter-drive can be kept closed, must start out in an open position when chop must be compensated for. In general, the backhand drive against chop is most often hit during an exchange of semi-chops or close-to-the-table half volleys, when one player may bring in a quick backhand drive which may very well score on the basis of surprise.

Against a long-range chop—one coming from, say, ten feet behind the table—there is almost never a case when the backhand drive would be more efficient to use than the forehand. A chop covering that distance will give the receiver ample time to step around his backhand side and hit the ball with his forehand wherever it may land.

For the backhand drive against chop use the stroke illustrated in Figure 27. Note the significantly longer backswing and the approach to the ball with the open-faced racket where the handle of the bat is pulled forward first, followed by the closing of the face of the bat as the wrist catches up and turns the blade over

Figure 27

The backhand drive

the top of the ball. Note, too, that having additional time against the slow-traveling chop, the player may make a pivot.

The backhand attack, as I have been stressing, is more or less the underprivileged and ignored stroke in the game. This is probably the reason that among the world-class players we find such a disparity of style in hitting this shot. The particular strokes I have illustrated above represent a composite of shots rather than the ideal stroke if, indeed, there is such a thing. Both Sido and Barna, the world champions I previously mentioned, hit what seemed to be the ideal backhand drive—yet each hit the shot quite differently.

The implication is that you can afford to be less rigid in learning this shot. Study the stroke I propose here and see if it works, but be prepared to experiment with small deviations too, for it may well be that you are the player destined to develop *the ideal backhand*. But don't bank on it. Table tennis is a forehand game as far as attack is concerned.

The Forehand Counter-Drive

Before the sponge bat came into general use in the mid-'50's, it was axiomatic that the most difficult shot in the game to bring off was a hard forehand counter-drive. To blast the ball with all of one's power and at the same time reverse the spin of one's opponent was the *ne plus ultra* of the sport. Even in master play it was considered a risky shot.

I recall that when I first saw the Japanese players Tanaka and Ogimura in 1955, each of whom subsequently won the world's singles title twice, I marveled at their ability to counter-drive with their forehands. They could intercept the ball close to the table and take it on the rise; or play it ten feet behind the table, taking it on the drop. But, in either case, they would hit the ball harder than I thought possible on a counter-drive. Later, when I learned to play with the sponge bat, I found that counter-driving with sponge is often the safest shot to make. With the sponge bat, as you have no doubt found, the ball is catapulted back toward the table as though it were fired from a sling. This, together with the extreme grip of the rubber, makes counter-driving simple and effective. It is small wonder that in the modern game almost all players prefer to attack and only rarely develop a fine defense. When the great Orientals, in particular, face each other they counter-drive on every point with such fury that rarely does the ball cross the net more than five or six times on any point.

Either of the forehand strokes you learned from this book, the European drive or my own, is appropriate for counter-driving. There are, however, a few suggestions I can make to speed your progress in developing the shot.

Counter-drives are made against topspinned balls that rebound higher from the table surface than balls that carry chop. So it is no longer possible to keep the elbow close to the body when hitting these shots. If a ball is being intercepted chest-high on your forehand side, your right elbow must be raised to that height prior to the backswing; for remember, the elbow is the hinge upon which the forearm swings.

Likewise, it is perfectly possible to counter-drive a ball that is arcing downward far behind the table and has almost touched the floor. Here, prior to the backswing, the upper arm and forearm must be straight and hanging vertically and the stroke delivered much like a bowling stroke.

Another general rule in counter-driving with the sponge bat (backhand or forehand) is that the harder you want to hit the ball the more you must close the face of the bat as you approach the ball; in other words the more *down* you must aim. Frequently you will find that when you get into a series of counter-driving exchanges you must aim downward more with each succeeding shot, until it seems as though you are aiming for the bottom of the net. But the harder you hit the ball the more of the catapult action you get—the sinking of the ball into the sponge and the subsequent thrust—and this must be compensated for.

Not every counter-drive, of course, requires hitting the ball as hard as possible. Indeed, some of the world's great players have developed a high, looping topspin, hit from deep backcourt and clearing the net sometimes by eight or nine feet. Though this shot is made with a counter-driving stroke, it would be more properly called a defensive lob. But when this shot hits the table, far from being a setup, the heavy topspin and high trajectory cause a high-bouncing ball that is extremely awkward to handle.

When developing your counter-drive, start off by practicing slow topspin exchanges, gradually increasing the tempo as you gain control. A counter-drive in match play is often a one-shot attempt that either wins or loses the point then and there. But it is a mistake to practice the shot in this way. Even shots of this advanced and difficult nature can be grooved if enough practice is devoted to half-speed play calculated to gain ball control.

Although the counter-driving exchanges at the highest level of play are the most dazzling and apparently inimitable shots of the game, the beginner should not postpone the development of this stroke. Even at the stage when a player is just learning the forehand drive he should, in every practice session, spend some time on the counter-drive. In the buddy system this merely requires that the players topspin at each other. The fact that ball control is difficult when one tries to counter-drive very hard should not dissuade even the beginner from practicing the shot. For one thing, five or ten minutes of each practice session spent in really blasting the ball will, despite the many errors, improve the forehand in general, for when the normal speed is resumed the ball will seem to be traveling much slower and the timing will be correspondingly easier. Another reason for developing the counter-drive early is that it cultivates an aggressive style of play. Too much reliance on defensive play, particularly success at winning games, will tend to mold the beginner into a defensive player, and while a player may win by being strictly defensive, in the long run an all-round game will be far better.

To the intermediate and perhaps even to the fairly advanced player it may seem obvious that the counter-drive style must be the most effective. "Are not the Orientals," they say, "the best players in the world, though they rarely play a defensive shot?" True enough. But the Orientals who play a one-wing game are the best players in the world *despite* their limitation. Their lack of defensive strokes derives from their penholder grip. Their forehand drives and counter-drives win for them because their attacking stroke is perfect and because they have incredible agility at covering the entire court with one side of the racket. But former world champion Ferenc Sido, who is six feet two and weighs 210 pounds, was not built for such acrobatics. Nonetheless, time after time in the Swaythling Cup, Sido defeated entire squads of Japanese. Sido planted his lumbering frame seven feet behind the table and chopped back the Japanese attack until, finding an opening, he ended the point with a sudden counter-drive off either wing. Against other styles, defensive players, for instance, Sido rarely backed away from the table. Thus he had *two* styles with which to win.

The Drop Shot

One of the concomitants of the change-over from normal rubber
bats to sponge bats was the disappearance of the drop shot from
the game. There are two reasons for this. First, the drop shot, a tiny
patting stroke which attempts to put the ball barely over the net,
must be made in answer to a chop. The purpose of the drop shot
is to surprise the opponent who is far behind the table with a ball
he cannot reach in time. The drop shot, therefore, presupposes that
your opponent is playing defense, and, as we have seen, defensive
play has gone out of fashion since the sponge. Second, the drop shot
requires a deft touch for its successful execution, and the sponge bat,
with its susceptibility to spin and its erratic behavior in general,
makes precision control impossible to attain. Thus, the vanishing
drop shot. There are times, however, when the drop shot is the
percentage play, and the student must have the shot in his repertoire.

A successful drop shot (a point winner) is almost always made
with the forehand. Since a good drop shot must come as a surprise,
your opponent must be led to expect an attacking stroke. Therefore,
a partial backswing as a feint is necessary. At best, the drop shot
is made almost as an impulse that occurs to one midway through
the preparation for a forehand drive.

The drop shot should almost always be placed on your opponent's
forehand. It is more difficult to stretch in over the table with the
forehand than with the backhand and if your opponent does reach
the shot, he is more likely to set the ball up on his return.

The drop shot is usually played as a pickup shot where the ball is
trapped just after the bounce and blocked over the net. Sometimes,
however, when your opponent is deep and out of position, the drop
shot may be made in answer to a setup as offering a better percentage than the kill shot. In this case, the drop shot is made by
taking the ball at the top of the bounce and allowing it merely to
touch the racket and fall.

In either case, whether it is played as a trap shot or hit at the top
of the bounce, the drop shot should never be made in answer to a
ball that has landed on your side of the table with depth. Only a
ball that drops shallow, close to the net, offers the chance for a
good drop shot. For, when one attempts to drop-shot a ball that has
fallen, say, six inches from the end of the table, so much forward

Figure 28

The drop shot

motion must be used to have the ball reach the net that it will carry well toward your oncoming opponent.

Figure 28 shows the pickup drop shot: *a* shows the feint of the forehand drive; *b* shows the change of direction of the swing; and *c* shows the position of wrist, forearm, and body just after contact.

CHAPTER 8

Tactics

Your arsenal of strokes is now complete. Your main assault weapon is your forehand drive and counter-drive. For prolonged sieges or in a temporary "fallback position," you have your backhand and forehand chopping game. For the infighting and skirmishes you have the table game. Develop these strokes perfectly and you may win the world championship. Even if your goal is somewhat more modest, with anything short of perfection of strokes, timing, footwork—the technical aspects of the game—you will still need to supplement your arsenal with winning plans. Just as a general charts his battle according to the equipment of his enemy, you will have to learn to adapt your game to the various styles of your opponents. No hard and fast rules can be laid down for this aspect of the game. It is here that your own competitive instincts and your ability to make correct on-the-spot decisions will manifest themselves as they lead to victory or defeat. After all, your opponent, too, may have studied this book and have come away with as fine a set of strokes as your own. At this point skill, to a certain extent, gives way to generalship.

There are many situations, of course, in which even superb generalship will not compensate for the disparity of skill between two players. But here are a few typical situations that all players, from beginners to experts, will encounter—situations in which tactics become crucial.

Playing Against the Blocker

Nothing is more disheartening to the player who is cultivating the strokes of the sport and has spent a good deal of time practicing them than to meet the sticky amateur who stands flush up to the table and, without spin or strokes, blocks every ball back like a stone wall. Losing to this type of player is much more frustrating than losing to an all-around good player, for the blocker lets you beat yourself. Players of this type have very few off days and never give a point away without a struggle. They must really be beaten.

In adapting your game to find a way to beat a blocker you have one very important advantage: once you find the way you will never lose to him again.

The first thing *not* to do against the blocker is to try to outsteady him at his own game. He has undoubtedly devoted his entire table-tennis career to perfecting his little patty-cake game and will certainly beat you at it. Nor will it do you much good to try to make him hit your chop into the net by spinning excessively hard. He will merely angle his racket higher and neutralize your spin.

What is needed to beat the blocker is the attack, primarily the forehand attack. The trouble is that the blocker puts the ball back so fast that you have very little time to get into position to hit your forehand. Undoubtedly the blocker will keep crowding you into your backhand corner of the table, and if you threaten to step around that shot all the way to your left, he will angle the ball to your extreme forehand. The blocker's advantage is the speed with which he returns the ball and his control over the position.

On the other hand, your advantage is that he is trapped up to the table and any hard-hit ball will force him into an error. Your only problem is how to force him into giving you a shot to kill.

The best procedure against him is as follows: On each point begin the exchange with a series of push shots. These can go anywhere on the table, as long as you give yourself time. Your objective will be to eventually step around a ball that he has hit to your backhand side and hit it hard with your forehand drive. Just before you do this, however, you should try to give him a slow traveling push shot, not too low, to his backhand—one that you have hit from your backhand. It is the slowness of your *own* shot that gives you the time to step around into your forehand position before his return. Now, if the blocker hits his backhand return to your forehand, his angle is limited, and you will have no trouble reaching it. Whether or not you can topspin it with any aggressiveness is another matter, but in any case you will not miss because of his having angled you out of position. If the blocker returns again to your backhand, you should be there—but in forehand position, waiting for the shot.

Your first attacking shot in the rally should be severe, not a kill, but hard enough to reasonably expect a loose return from him. To force this loose return, your attacking shot should not only be severe but it should be—and this is crucial—well-placed. The blocker, remember, though he may return the ball quickly and put you under pressure, also is vulnerable to the quick hit because he has committed himself to a close-to-the-table game and does not retreat. Therefore, any shot that surprises him will force a setup or an error. The most vulnerable spot on the table for a blocker is the spot between his forehand and his backhand, the break-off point at which he must switch from his backhand side (practically all blockers play backhand games) to his forehand side. Any shot hit from your backhand side with severity to that mid-point in the blocker's position will force the setup, but I recommend hitting this shot with your forehand from your backhand corner—what we would call a forehand straight down the line.

If the blocker does manage to keep the ball low on this return, preventing you from putting it away, don't gamble by trying for the kill anyway. Too many players pledge themselves to an idea and forget they are playing against an opponent. Be flexible. If your opponent returns your first attacking shot low, start the maneuver all over again—first the series of half volleys, then the slow, deep ball to the backhand, then the try for the attacking shot to force the setup.

If you keep picking on that in-between spot of the blocker's defense, the mid-point between his backhand and forehand, where essentially he can hit neither shot comfortably, the blocker will no doubt begin to position himself differently. You should notice him gradually shifting toward his right to give himself more coverage with his backhand. Pretty soon, to find his mid-point, you will have to hit the ball so far to his forehand side that you are in danger of hitting the ball off the side of the table toward your left. Now is the time to make your first attacking shot to his backhand, and, if possible do so, with just the slightest preliminary feint of hitting to the forehand. Remember, the blocker is trapped only if you can force the setup. To force the setup, you must hit your shots to the right place in order to open up the entire court.

You should have no trouble putting away the setup. You can hit it anywhere—but hit it hard! Against blockers I usually put the ball away right down the center, straight at them, varying the kill now and then to the sides.

You may lose, of course, when playing a particular blocker in this forcing fashion, but your compensation is that once you can win a few games by this method, he will never win another game no matter how long he plays you. His only advantage is one of style, and once you solve that, winning becomes no problem. The passivity of the blocker must yield to your attack if your stroke is sound.

Playing Against the Basher

There is always that fellow who puts his head down, serves, top-spins one or two balls at you and then . . . pow! He either hits a kill through you or hits the ball into the seats. This type of fellow is usually quick and nervous and impatient, and often, under the pressure of a close score, will blow sky-high.

There is not too much you can do against him, since he is determined to make or break the game himself. My own particular game always employed a low, heavy chop defense, and more often than not these bashers beat themselves when they played me. In their impatience to have the point done with they were constantly swinging at nearly impossible shots.

If a basher is beating himself you do not have to worry, but when his shots begin scoring all around you it is time to adjust. Maybe you *can* do something to stop him.

The obvious method is to fight him for the attack, force him back if possible. Well, if you can do that you are a better basher than he is, and you will win. But how can you stop him otherwise? A system I have often used successfully (not that I haven't lost a few games to bashers) when I begin to see those kill shots going through me is to try to groove the ball right down the middle of the table, floating it in low rather than trying for the stiff chop. Very often during a match the attacker may miss wildly for the first game or two, hitting your chops into the net or your change-up "nothing balls" off the ends. But when he gets warmed up, his aim will get better and then you had better have a plan.

This plan of mine—grooving the ball down the center without too much spin—is designed to neutralize the basher's best shot and prey on his temperament as well. By putting the ball down the center you reduce the angle he can get on his smashes. Frequently, blasting forehand players hit their best and hardest shots from their backhand side (with their forehands) to your backhand side, and it is a tactical blunder to try to force them into that backhand corner. Their subsequent angle to your backhand can be too much to cope with. Likewise, a defensive shot played to their forehand side gives them the angle cross-court to your forehand. But the middle shot gives them almost no severe angle.

Additionally, the idea of taking off some of the spin is designed to increase your accuracy. Once the attacker has got the range of your chop, and is able to judge it accurately, he has the advantage. It is better now for you to switch to a floating ball with less backspin and try to unnerve him with consistency. His impatience often works for you and, of course, he will be distressed at the fact that the center ball gives him no angle to pass your defense.

At the London World Championships in 1954 I used this system against Japan's number-two man, Tomita, a crashing penholder with a bombing forehand. In the quarter finals of the men's singles I was leading 2–0 in games and had a 12–8 point lead in the third game. Nine more points would have put me in the semifinals. Tomita tied the score with four brilliant shots through my backhand defense and I switched to my center theory. Tomita didn't even notice. His forehand by this time was so warmed up that not even my grooving the ball down the center could contain it. So I shook hands as a loser despite a good theory.

Beating the Topspin Artist

If in developing your game you acquire a tendency to be passive, to let attacking players force you on the defense and defensive players force you to attack, you will always be playing against players who are playing *their* game, not yours. You may win this way, to be sure, just by being better, but you will face many problem situations. One of the most difficult to solve occurs when a medium-speed attacking player forces you on the defense and, without trying for the kill shot like the basher, is content to topspin and topspin until he forces you into an error. It might seem that because you are playing defensively you should be steadier than the attacker, but this is not always the case.

When I played the great Czech player, Ivan Andreadis, at the Tokyo World Championships, I had already lost to him in our two previous meetings. He seemed to have my number. Ivan would stand right in the center of the court, two or three feet behind the table, and topspin me to death. My normal heavy chop, so effective against the crashers, meant little to him. He merely aimed higher to compensate for the spin and kept me back on the defense. Eventually, I would chop into the net or off the end. Only rarely did he pass me or hit the ball hard. He was seeded No. 1 at the Tokyo Worlds and I badly wanted to avenge the previous defeats. I decided on a daring plan. I resolved that I would not play my own game, but would imitate the style of certain players who gave Andreadis trouble. Those players were all long-range defensive players who floated the ball in without much spin—Leach, Bergmann, and a few sticky French players.

Armed with this plan, I played the first ten points against Andreadis completely passively, trying only to match his steadiness with my own determination—a determination not to score points by severity but rather by outlasting him.

It must have been as frustrating for Andreadis as it was for me; I refused to miss by chopping hard, and he refused to gamble. When I felt I had his mild attack under control I even hazarded setting the ball up a bit higher just to bait him. Sure enough, when he saw that I was not going to try to chop him down as he had expected, he became overly aggressive and little by little my lead increased and his patience vanished. I won in straight games.

More recently, that great defensive artist, Eberhard Scholer of Germany, has used this passive technique to perfection. He is anathema to the Japanese "loopers," because when playing them he retreats and waits patiently for them to beat themselves.

(The loop, I should explain, is an excessively spun topspin shot in which all the force of the stroke is directed upward to achieve the spin. The ball has forward motion, too, but primarily it is the severe spin that utterly confounds a player not accustomed to it. I have not illustrated it in this book because it has, in my opinion, destroyed many potentially fine attacking players through its overuse. The Japanese, when they were the world champions, developed the loop and, for a time, increased their superiority with it. But soon everyone had learned to play against it and the Japanese began to lose matches. It seemed that what they had done was to spend so much time training their players to loop that they had lost their forehand drive by substituting one for the other. As a consequence China moved up into the number-one spot. The Chinese *never* loop. They attack! The loop, incidentally, can be executed only with the inverted sponge bat.)

Beating the Chiseler

In table tennis argot a "chiseler" is a strictly defensive player— a player who almost never takes a chance. This is the kind of player who delights in playing against topspin artists or attacking players who lack the extra bit of steam to penetrate a solid defense.

Up until the mid-1950's when the Orientals firmly established their supremacy, the chiselers in table tennis did very well. Often there were one or two first-class chiselers still hanging around in the quarter finals of the world tourney. But when the Orientals got going, they were demolishing the opposition, chiselers and attackers alike, in the early rounds, and when major tournaments were reduced to the last eight players, frequently only Chinese, Japanese, or North Koreans remained. This is not to the particular discredit of the chiselers, who, as I say, fared no worse than the attackers, but the Orientals did show a style that beat the chiselers convincingly. Power was the style.

Well, this was really not new. Way back in 1948 at the London World Championships, Marty Reisman, a fellow New Yorker, and I were blasting the ball so hard and ending the points so quickly that the International Table Tennis Federation seriously proposed that the net be raised to 6½ inches to slow up the "American style" which, it claimed, was detrimental to the sport. In the light of later developments—the sponge and its excessive speed—this now seems absurd, but I mention it to illustrate that speed, as a crushing weapon against defensive players, is not new. If you hit the ball hard enough and consistently enough, the defensive player cannot win.

This advantage of the attacker, however, is largely theoretical. In match play the defensive player has a number of distinct practical advantages over the attacker. First of all, the attacker usually takes longer to warm up in a match. The extra power he uses and the smaller margin of safety on his shots call for correspondingly greater control and quite often he does not acquire this until well along in the match. Sometimes, indeed, his drives begin to find the range too late.

In this connection one must bear in mind that table-tennis scoring is particularly disadvantageous to a slow starter. If the attacker, in trying to warm up his game, falls behind at the beginning of a game so that the score is 6 or 7 to 1, he may as well kiss that game good-by. Against a solid defensive player he cannot reasonably expect his percentage to be good enough in the remaining points. So, if he loses the first game, he is already one third out of the match in a best of five or, worse, half out of it in a two out of three game match. Compare this to the scoring system in lawn tennis, where the basic unit, the game, is won by scoring only four points, and there are six games in each set, and three sets decide a match. Under this system the slower starter with basically greater ability does not suffer so much. If, at the outset of a match, he wastes a few games to warm up his shots, he can still win the major unit, the set, whenever his shots begin to click.

The chiseler has another practical advantage: he is much less apt to have off days. Again, the point is that to hit the ball really hard requires perfect control. Unfamiliar playing conditions, a ball that is slightly wobbly, or the slightest draft in an arena will result in a slight loss of control and consequently affect the attacker more than the defender. Thus one can see that these practical advantages of the chiseler often compensate fully for his theoretical disadvantage of passivity.

How can the attacker increase his advantage against the defensive player?

If the attacker has learned a sound stroke he can at least hit the ball hard. His control is another matter, but he should realize that his main weapon is speed and he should use it. There are no worse tactics for the aggressive player to employ than to be timid or over cautious. The timid hitter allows the defensive player to grind him down in a protracted struggle that, as it progresses, more and more favors the defender. The attacker must realize that the defender, too, gets warmed up in a match. Even against a power hitter the defender will, after a few games, begin retrieving some of his outright kill shots. Usually he cannot retrieve enough kill shots to make any significant difference once the power hitter has found the range, but against a timid attacker, one who is never quite sure whether to go for the kill when the opportunity is offered or to play it safe with a topspin shot, the defender gets stronger and stronger in a match. Against this kind of quasi-attacking play the chiseler often seems, after half a game or so, to have the ball tied to a string, so accustomed does he become to the topspinner's pace and rhythm.

The attacker's main weapon, therefore, must be speed. When playing the chiseler his object on every point should be to force the loose ball—the ball that comes back just a bit higher than the others—as soon as possible, and then go for the kill. Mind you, the loose ball is not an outright setup. Waiting for the out-and-out "meatball" before trying for the kill is tactically poor for the reasons outlined above. The attacker must expect to miss a certain number of shots; his main concern should be to keep the percentage in his favor.

Hitting the ball with full power requires the utmost confidence. The attacker is doomed as soon as he begins to choke up on his drives. But full confidence on the power shots is, of course, much more than mere mental attitude. The confidence is built on experience—the memory of hitting the same shot countless times before, in the same way, and having it find its mark. Therefore, when facing the prospect of a match with a chiseler, I recommend that the attacker pay particular attention to his pre-match warm-up (the warm-up on the practice tables if he is playing in a tournament). Here he should refresh his memory of hitting kill shots by having someone feed him setups while he blasts away at them.

As I mentioned above, the attacker takes longer to warm up than does the defensive player; so, for attacking players, I recommend about an hour's warm-up just before a match. More matches are lost through being cold than through being tired. Moreover, because of the sustained action in table tennis and the close quarters of match play, table tennis is a nerve-wracking game to play when there is a lot at stake. A long warm-up before a match, almost long enough to be fatiguing, helps dissipate excess nervous energy.

Though his main weapon is power, the attacker should try, too, to increase his efficiency by driving to the right places on the table. If he is up against a defensive player with a weaker backhand than forehand, for instance, obviously he will work on the backhand side. But assuming the defensive player is equally strong on both wings (as is most often the case) the attacker should not lose sight of the positional possibilities.

The shot that I have always found effective against any defense is the center shot—a drive hit directly at the player. This is the defensive player's most vulnerable spot, his stomach, for a shot hit there with sufficient pace gives him no time to pivot for either a backhand or a forehand chop and the result is often an improvised scoop that comes back as a "meatball." Hitting to the corners, of course, gives the attacker more angle and length, and thus more safety, but the center shot makes up for its greater risk by having to be hit with less power to be effective.

Very often during a match the attacker finds the range early and gets off to a good lead only to find, after a game or so, that the chiseler has tightened up his defense and is getting the ball back more consistently. This can often be the turning point of a match, for unless the attacker can summon up more power to penetrate the defense he is in danger. Rather than trying for the extra power, his best chance now is to break up the defense.

Breaking up the defense simply means changing the pace. The defender gets warmed up too, remember, and even the hardest drives can be handled once the chiseler finds the rhythm. When this happens, good tactics require that the attacker mix things up a little. Instead of applying constant pressure with topspin shots designed to force a loose ball that can be killed, the attacker should vary the points by utilizing the half volley, the drop shot, and even a few points played defensively. This should not be construed as cowardice or as showing that the defensive player now has the match under control. It is merely a way in which the attacker takes the match out of a pattern that is worsening for him. By slowing up the game temporarily, the attacker takes the defender out of his groove and, hopefully, when the attacker again assumes his aggressive role, the defender will be not quite so steady.

Some of the game's most effective attackers, by the way, are players without a particularly bullet-like kill shot. But they make up for this by having their topspin shots (their build-up shots, in other words) relatively slow, so that it is the change of pace between the build-up and the kill, rather than the speed of the kill shot itself, that makes their game effective.

Though experts are inclined to dub most defensive players chiselers, the fact is that real chiselers (players who never attack at all—who are, indeed, incapable of attacking because they don't know how) are not seen in modern competition. The chiseler without any attacking stroke at all can be beaten simply and effectively just by putting him under the disadvantage of playing under the so-called "expedite rule." This rule, first devised by the Americans but now used internationally, sets a unique time limit on matches. Whenever a game is unfinished after fifteen minutes of play the expedite rule is invoked by the referee. Under this rule, each player, on his own service, has thirteen shots (including the serve) in which to end the point. If the receiver returns the server's thirteenth shot the point is awarded to the receiver. The serve alternates after each point.

Obviously, against an all-out chiseler, all a reasonably capable attacking player (or even a defensive player) has to do is to push the ball back and forth with the chiseler for fifteen minutes. Even if the score after fifteen minutes is something like 6–1 in favor of the chiseler the attacker will soon make up the deficit under the expedite rule as the chiseler will lose *all* the points on which he serves.

Even in the modern sponge game with its furious speed and counter-driving exchanges, defensive players still exist and to beat them often requires invoking the expedite rule. Only the Asians seem to be able to power their way through any defense.

There is nothing shameful about winning a tournament match under the expedite rule. It is a fine rule designed to prevent those interminable seven-hour matches that plagued the sport back in the 1930's when two chiselers could push the ball back and forth for hours and bore the paying spectators half to death in the process. The only important thing to remember is that often the expedite rule can backfire. Because a player seems to prefer to play defensively does not always mean that he cannot attack. Too often a player tries to play for the expedite rule, succeeds in getting it invoked, and finds that he is worse off than before because the apparent chiseler, when absolutely *forced* to, can attack very well.

International Laws
of Table Tennis

1. The Table

The table shall be in surface rectangular, 9 ft. in length, 5 ft. in width; it shall be supported in such a way that its upper surface shall be 2 ft. 6 in. above the floor, and shall lie in a horizontal plane.

It shall be made of any material and shall yield a uniform bounce of not less than 8¾ in. and not more than 9¾ in. when a standard ball, preferably of medium bounce, is dropped from a height of 12 in. above its surface.

The upper surface of the table shall be termed the "playing surface"; it shall be matt, colour very dark, preferably dark green, with a white line ¾ in. broad along each edge.

The lines at the edges or ends of the playing surface shall be termed "end lines." The lines at the edges or sides of the playing surface shall be termed "side lines."

2. The Net and Its Supports

The playing surface shall be divided into two courts of equal size by a net running parallel to the end lines and 4 ft. 6 in. from each. The net, with its suspension, shall be 6 ft. in length; its upper part along its whole length shall be 6 in. above the playing surface; its lower part along the whole length shall be close to the playing surface. The net shall be suspended by a cord attached at each end to an upright post 6 in. high; the outside limits of each post shall be 6 in. outside the side line.

3. The Ball

The ball shall be spherical. It shall be made of celluloid or a similar plastic, white or yellow and matt; it shall not be less than 1.46 in. nor more than 1.50

in. in diameter; it shall not be less than 2.40 gr. nor more than 2.53 gr. in weight.

4. The Racket

The racket may be of any size, shape, or weight. Its surface shall be dark coloured and matt. The blade shall be continuous, of even thickness, flat and rigid. If the blade is covered on either side, this covering may be either— of plain, ordinary pimpled rubber, with pimples outward, of a total thickness of not more than 2 mm.; or— of "sandwich," consisting of a layer of cellular rubber surfaced by plain ordinary pimpled rubber—turned outwards or inwards—in which case the total thickness of covering of either side shall not be more than 4 mm.

When rubber is used on both sides of a racket, the colour need not be similar: when wood is used for either side, or for both sides, it should be dark, either naturally, or by being stained (not painted) in such a way as not to change the friction-character of its surface.

Note: The part of the blade nearest the handle and gripped by the fingers may be covered with cork or other materials for convenience of grip; it is to be regarded as part of the handle.

Note: If the reverse side of the racket is never used for striking the ball, it may all be of cork or any other material convenient for gripping. The limitation of racket cover materials refers only to the striking surface. A stroke with a side covered with cork or any other gripping surface would, however, be illegal and result in a lost point.

Note: Each side of the blade, whether used for striking the ball or not, must be of a uniform dark colour.

5. The Order of Play: Definitions

The player who first strikes the ball during a rally shall be termed the server.

The player who next strikes the ball during a rally shall be termed the receiver.

The server shall first make a good service, the receiver shall then make a good return, and thereafter server and receiver shall each alternately make a good return.

The period during which the ball is in play shall be termed a rally.

A rally the result of which is not scored shall be termed a let.

A rally the result of which is scored shall be termed a point.

6. A Good Service

The ball shall be placed on the palm of the free hand, which must be stationary, open and flat, and above the level of the playing surface. Service shall commence by the server projecting the ball by hand only, without imparting spin, near vertically upwards (see diagram), so that the ball is visible at all times to the umpire, and so that it visibly leaves the palm. As the ball is then descending from the height of its trajectory, it shall be struck so that it touch first the server's court and then, passing directly over or around the net, touch the receiver's court.

THE NEW SERVICE RULE ADOPTED FOR USE AS FROM
JULY 1st 1967

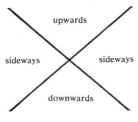

(See 6. A Good Service)

Note: Missed Service: Note that, if a player, in attempting to serve, miss the ball altogether, it is a lost point because the ball was in play from the moment it left his hand and a good service has not been made of the ball already in play.

Definitions for above:

"Struck": "Struck" means "hit with the racket or with the racket hand" which, for this purpose, shall be understood as included in the racket. The racket hand is the hand carrying the racket; the free open hand is the hand not carrying racket. Therefore, a return effected with the hand alone, after dropping the racket, is "not good" for it is no longer the "racket hand"; a return effected by the racket alone, after it has slipped or been thrown from the hand, is likewise "not good," for the ball is not "struck."

The phrase Table Surface (comprising the courts) is to be interpreted as including the top edges of the table-top, and a ball in play which strikes these latter is therefore good and still in play; though if it strikes the side of the table-top below the edge, it becomes dead and counts against the last striker.

The direction in which the ball is travelling since it was last struck, its spin, and the direction in which it rebounds from the edge can all help to distinguish between a "good" ball that has touched the edge and a "bad" ball that has made contact below the edge. If the point of contact of the ball has occurred at the end or side of the table away from the striker it must nearly always have been a "good" touch; only exceptionally heavy spin could have brought about a contact completely below the edge. If the contact has occurred on the same side of the table as that from which the ball was struck, it may, however, have occurred below the edge and if the rebound in this case is directly downward this is a sign that the contact must have been "bad," i.e. against the side, below the edge.

If the ball, in passing over the net, or around the net, touch it or its supports it shall, nevertheless, be considered to have passed directly. "Around the net" shall be considered as being under or around the projection of the net and supports outside the side line. The net end should be close enough to the post to prevent the ball from passing between net and post and to pass so would not constitute "around the net."

The free hand, while in contact with the ball in service, shall be open, with the fingers together, thumb free and the ball resting on the palm without being cupped or pinched in any way by the fingers.

7. A Good Return

A ball having been served or returned in play shall be struck so that it pass directly over or around the net and touch directly the opponent's court, provided that, if the ball, having been served or returned in play, return with its own impetus over or around the net, it may be struck, while still in play, so that it touch directly the opponent's court.

8. In Play

The ball is in play from the moment at which it is projected from the hand in service until:—

It has touched one court twice consecutively.

It has, except in service, touched each court alternately without having been struck by the racket intermediately.

It has been struck by either player more than once consecutively.

It has touched either player or anything that he wears or carries, except his racket or his racket hand below the wrist.

On the volley it come in contact with the racket or the racket hand below the wrist.

It has touched any object other than the net, supports, or those referred to above.

It has, under the Expedite System, been returned by thirteen successive good returns of the receiving player or pair.

9. A Let

The rally is a let:—

If the ball served in passing over the net touch it or its supports, provided the service either be otherwise good or be volleyed by the receiver.

Definition: The Volley: If the ball in play come into contact with the racket or racket hand, not yet having touched the playing surface on one side of the net since last being struck on the other side, it shall be said to have been volleyed.

If a service be delivered when the receiver is not ready, provided always that he may not be deemed to be unready if he attempt to strike at the ball.

If either player be prevented by an accident, not under his control, from serving a good service or making a good return.

If either player lose the point owing to an accident not within his control.

If it be interrupted for correction of a mistake in playing order or ends.

If it be interrupted for application of the Expedite System.

If it be interrupted by the intrusion of another ball in the playing area.

Ball Fractured in Play

If the ball split or become otherwise fractured in play, affecting a player's return, the rally is a let. It is the umpire's duty to stop play, recording a let, when he has reason to believe that the ball in play is fractured or imperfect; and to decide those cases in which the faulty ball is clearly fractured in actually going out of play, and in no way handicaps the player's return, when the point should be scored. In all cases of doubt, however, he should declare a let.

10. A Point

Either player shall lose a point:—

If he fail to make a good service.

If a good service or a good return having been made by his opponent, he fail to make a good return.

If he, or his racket, or anything that he wears or carries touch the net or its supports while the ball is in play.

If he, or his racket, or anything that he wears or carries, move the playing surface while the ball is in play.

If his free hand touch the playing surface while the ball is in play.

If, before the ball in play shall have passed over the end lines or side lines not yet having touched the playing surface on his side of the table since being struck by his opponent, it come in contact with him or with anything that he wears or carries.

If at any time he volley the ball.

Expedite System

If a game be unfinished fifteen minutes after it has begun, the rest of that game and the remaining games of the match shall proceed under the Expedite System. Thereafter, each player shall serve one service in turn and, if the service and twelve following strokes of the server are returned by good returns of the receiver, the server shall lose the point.

If time was called during a rally, the player who served that rally shall serve first. If time was called between rallies, the receiver of the last rally shall serve next.

11. A Game

A game shall be won by the player who first wins 21 points, unless both players shall have scored 20 points, when the winner of the game shall be he who first wins two points more than his opponent.

12. A Match

A match shall consist of one game or the best of three or best of five games.

Play shall be continuous throughout, except that either opposing player is entitled to claim a repose period of not more than five minutes' duration between the third and fourth games of a five-game match, and of one minute between any other successive games.

Note: This rule defines a contest between two players or pairs. A contest consisting of a group of individual matches between two sides is usually distinguished as a "team match."

13. The Choice of Ends and Service

The choice of ends and the right to be server or receiver in every match shall be decided by toss, provided that, if the winner of the toss choose the right to be server or receiver, the other player shall have the choice of ends, and vice-versa, and provided that the winner of the toss may, if he prefer it, require the other player to make the first choice.

14. The Change of Ends and Service

Ends

The player who started at one end in a game shall start at the other in the immediately subsequent game, and so on, until the end of the match. In the last possible game of the match the players shall change ends when first either player reaches the score 10.

Service

After five points the receiver shall become the server, and the server the receiver, and so on after each five points until the end of the game or the score 20-all, or if the game be interrupted under the Expedite System. From the score 20-all, or if the game be interrupted under Expedite System, the service shall change after each point until the end of the game. The player who served first in a game shall be receiver first in the immediately subsequent game, and so on until the end of a match.

15. Out of Order of Ends or Service

Ends

If the players have not changed ends when ends should have been changed, the players shall change ends as soon as the mistake is discovered, unless a game has been completed since the error, when the error shall be ignored. In any circumstances, all points scored before the discovery shall be reckoned.

Service

If a player serve out of his turn, play shall be interrupted as soon as the mistake is discovered and shall continue with that player serving who, according to the sequence established at the beginning of the match, should be the server at the score that has been reached. In any circumstances, all points scored before the discovery shall be reckoned.

DOUBLES

16. The above Laws shall apply in the Doubles Game except as below.

17. The Table

The surface of the table shall be divided into two parts by a white line ⅛ in. broad, running parallel with the side lines and distant equally from each of them. This line shall be termed the centre line.

Note: The doubles centre line may be permanently marked in full length on the table. This is a convenience and in no way invalidates the table for singles play.

The part of the table surface on the nearer side of the net and the right of the centre line in respect to the server shall be called the server's right half-court, that on the left in respect to him the server's left half-court. The part of the table surface on the farther side of the net and the left of the centre line in respect to the server shall be called the receiver's right half-court, that on the right in respect to the server the receiver's left half-court.

18. A Good Service

The service shall be delivered as otherwise provided, and so that it touch first the server's right half-court or the centre line on his side of the net, and then passing directly over or around the net, touch the receiver's right half-court or the centre line on his side of the net.

19. The Order of Play

The server shall first make a good service, the receiver shall then make a good return, the partner of the server shall then make a good return, the partner of the receiver shall then make a good return, the server shall then make a good return and thereafter each player alternately in that sequence shall make a good return.

20. The Choice of the Order of Play

The pair who have the right to serve the first five services in any game shall decide which partner shall do so. In the first game of a match the opposing pair shall then decide similarly which shall be the first receiver. In subsequent games the serving pair shall choose their first server and the first receiver will then be established automatically to correspond with the first server as provided below.

21. The Order of Service

Throughout each game, except as provided in the second paragraph, the first five services shall be delivered by the selected partner of the pair who have the right to do so and shall be received by the appropriate partner of the opposing pair. The second five services shall be delivered by the receiver of the first five services and received by the partner of the server of the first five services. The third five services shall be delivered by the partner of the server of the first five services and received by the partner of the receiver of the first five services. The fourth five services shall be delivered by the partner of the receiver of the first five services and received by the server of the first five services. The fifth five services shall be delivered as the first five services. And so on, in sequence, until the end of the game or the score 20-all or the introduction of the Expedite System, when the sequence of serving and receiving shall be uninterrupted, but each player shall serve only one service in turn until the end of the game.

In the last possible game of a match when first either player reaches the score 10 the receiving pair must alter its order of serving.

In each game of a match the initial order of receiving shall be opposite to that in the preceding game.

22. Out of Order of Receiving

If a player act as receiver out of his turn play shall be interrupted as soon as the mistake is discovered and shall continue with that player receiving who, according to the sequence established at the beginning of the game or at the score 10 if that sequence has been changed, should be receiver at the score which has been reached. In any circumstances all points scored before the discovery shall be reckoned.